XETER - EXMOUTH

JDLEIGH SALTERTON · EXMINSTER · WES

C000089299

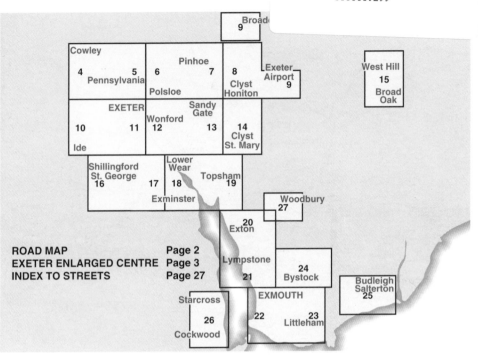

ROAD MAP	Page 2
EXETER ENLARGED CENTRE	Page 3
INDEX TO STREETS	Page 27

Every effort has been made to verify the accuracy of information in this book but the publishers cannot accept responsibility for expense or loss caused by an error or omission. Information that will be of assistance to the user of the maps will be welcomed.

The representation on these maps of a road, track or path is no evidence of the existence of a right of way.

Car Park	P
Public Convenience	C
Place of Worship	+
One-way Street	→
Pedestrianized	
Post Office	●

Scale of street plans 4 inches to 1 mile
Unless otherwise stated

Street plans prepared and published by ESTATE PUBLICATIONS, Bridewell House, TENTERDEN, KENT, and based upon the ORDNANCE SURVEY mapping with the permission of The Controller of H. M. Stationery Office.

The Publishers acknowledge the co-operation of the local authorities of towns represented in this atlas.

Stockleigh English · Cheriton Fitzpaine · Colebrook · Dulford · Kers
Village · A3072 · Cadbury · A396 · M5 · Mutterton · Westcott · A373
Sandford · Upton Hellions · Stockleigh Pomeroy · Up Exe · **Bradninch** · Plymtree · Norman's Green
Thorverton · **Silverton** · Hele · Langford · Clyst Hydon
Shobrooke · Efford · Nether Exe · Rewe · Budlake · Clyst St Lawrence · Higher Tale
Crediton · R. Yeo · Brampford Speke · R. Culm · Westwood · Talaton · Fer · R. Tale
Uton · A377 · Hookway · Newton St Cyres · Upton Pyne · Stoke Canon · **Broadclyst** · **Whimple**
Cowley · R. Exe · Poltimore · Dog Village · Fairmile
Tedburn St Mary · A396 · **EXETER** · Pinhoe · Rockbeare · B3174 · **West Hill**
Whitestone · Pennsylvania · Whipton · Clyst Honiton · Marsh Green · Broad Oak
A30 · Longdown · Polsloe · Sowton · A30 · Venn Ottery
B3212 · Ide · Wonford · Sandy Gate · **EXETER SERVICES** · Farringdon · Harpford · A3052
nstord · Alphington · Countess Wear · Clyst St Mary · Woodbury Salterton · **New Popple**
Shillingford St George · Lower Wear · 31 · M5 · Clyst St George · Woodbury · Hawkerland · B3180
Dunchideock · **Exminster** · **Topsham** · Ebford · B3179 · Colaton Raleigh
ford · Doddiscombsleigh · Kennford · Exton · Yettington · R. Otter
Christow · Higher Ashton · Kenn · Powderham · Lympstone · East Budleigh · Otte
Lower Ashton · Kenton · Bystock · B3178
Trusham · A380 · A379 · Starcross · **EXMOUTH** · Littleham · **Budleigh Salterton**
Hennock · B3193 · Cockwood · B3178
Bovey Tracey · **Chudleigh** · Ashcombe
Chudleigh Knighton · Ideford · Luton · **Dawlish** · Dawlish Warren
Heathfield · Preston · Bishopsteignton · Holcombe · A379
deast · A38 · Teigngrace · River Teign · **Teignmouth**
Kingsteignton · Shaldon
NEWTON ABBOT · Netherton · Combeinteignhead · Stokeinteignhead
West Ogwell · Haccombe
East Ogwell · A381 · A380 · Coffinswell · Maidencombe
Denbury · Abbotskerswell
Ipplepen · **Kingskerswell** · Barton

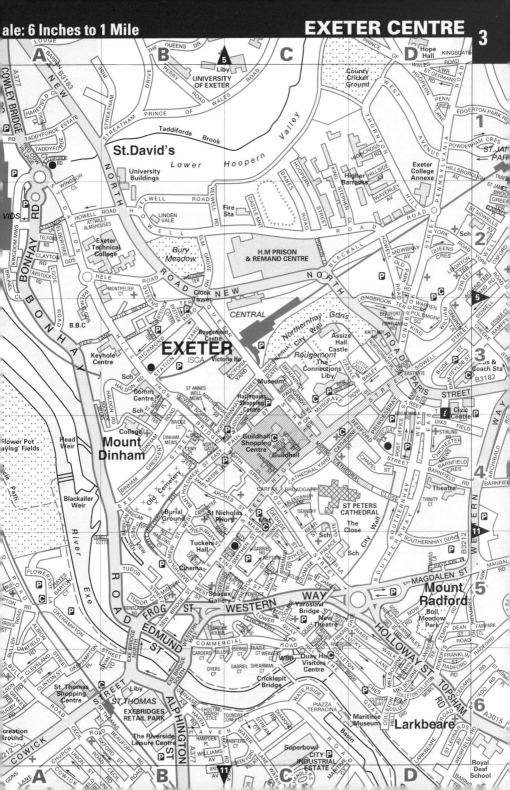

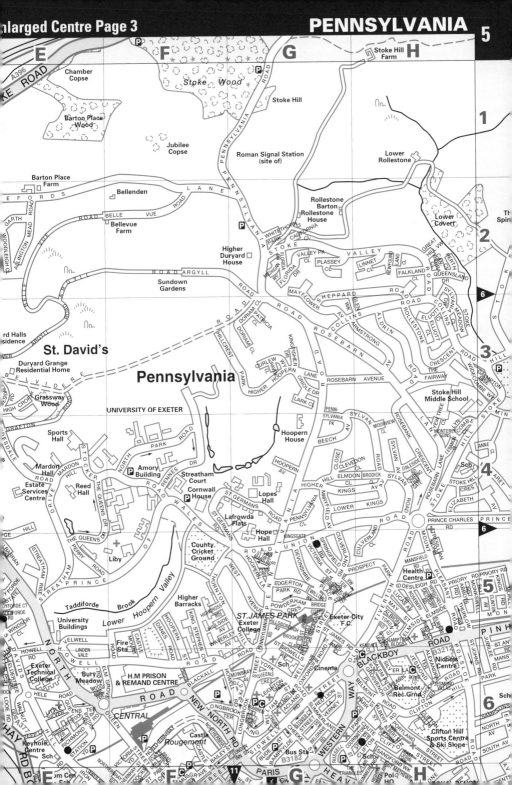

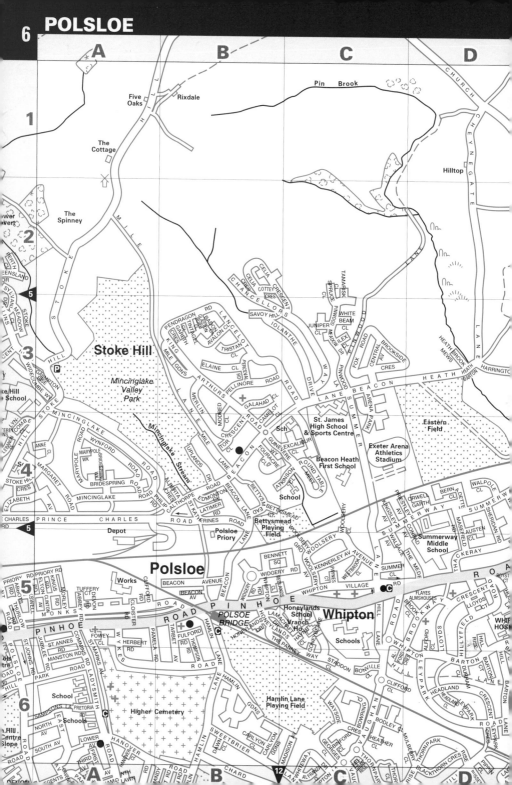

Kerswell Barton

Brockhill

Wishford Farm

STATION

HELLINGS

PARK LANE

TRADING ESTATE

HUNGRY FOX ESTATE

Clyst Valley

MOSSHAYNE LANE

Shermoor Farm

COTTERELL RD

SHERCROFT CL

Mosshayne

MOSSHAYNE

Works

ROAD

Hayes Farm

TITHEBARN LANE

LANE

MILL LANE

WATERSLADE LANE

BLACKHORSE

ENDSLEIGH CRES

Clyst Honiton Bridge

SHIP LANE

ST MICHAELS

ST MICHAELS HILL

CHURCH SIDE

Clyst Honiton
Sch

HONITON

RD

HONITON RD

A30

ROAD

Home Farm

B3184

Sowton Brake

SOWTON LANE

Marlborough Farm

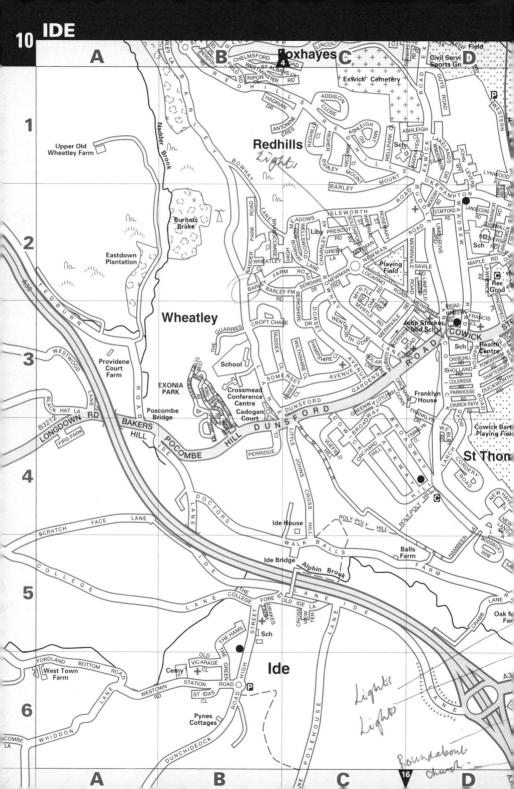

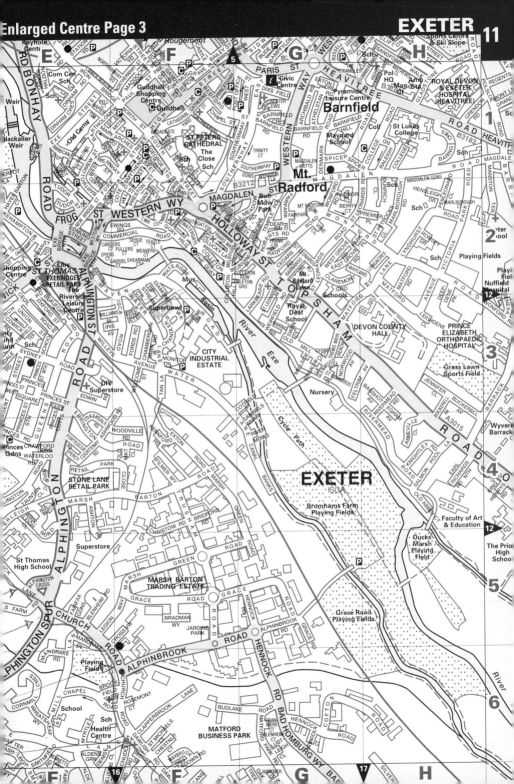

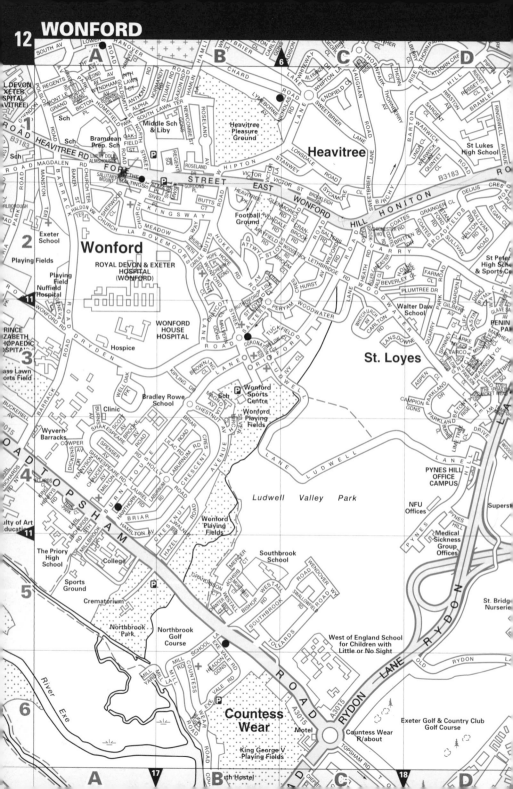

Heavitree

Wonford

St. Loyes

Countess Wear

ROYAL DEVON & EXETER HOSPITAL (WONFORD)

WONFORD HOUSE HOSPITAL

Ludwell Valley Park

PYNES HILL OFFICE CAMPUS

Exeter Golf & Country Club Golf Course

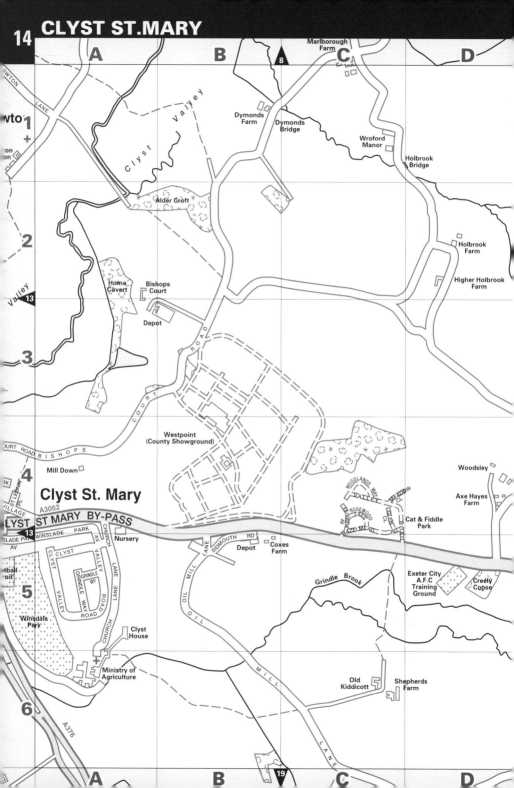

A   B   8   C   D

Marlborough Farm

Newton

Newton Lane

1 +

on on

Clyst valley

Dymonds Farm

Dymonds Bridge

Wroford Manor

Holbrook Bridge

Alder Croft

2

Valley 13

Holbrook Farm

Higher Holbrook Farm

Home Covert

Bishops Court

Depot

ROAD

3

COURT

Westpoint (County Showground)

Mill Down

COURT ROAD BISHOPS

4

Clyst St. Mary

A3052

CLYST ST MARY BY-PASS

13

SLADE PARK AV

WINSLADE PARK AV

Woodsley

Axe Hayes Farm

WOODLANDS WAY

VALLEY

ROSEWOOD CRES

MEADOW CL

HAZELMEAD

Cat & Fiddle Park

PARK AV

CHURCH LANE AV

VALLEY LANE

Nursery

CLYST

GRINDLE WY

GRINDLE WAY

VALLEY ROAD

CHURCH LANE ROAD

SIDMOUTH RD

Depot

Coxes Farm

Grindle Brook

Exeter City A.F.C Training Ground

Creely Copse

5

Football Ground

Winslade Park

Clyst House

OIL MILL LANE

OIL

MILL

Ministry of Agriculture

Old Kiddicott

Shepherds Farm

6

A376

LANE

A   B   19   C   D

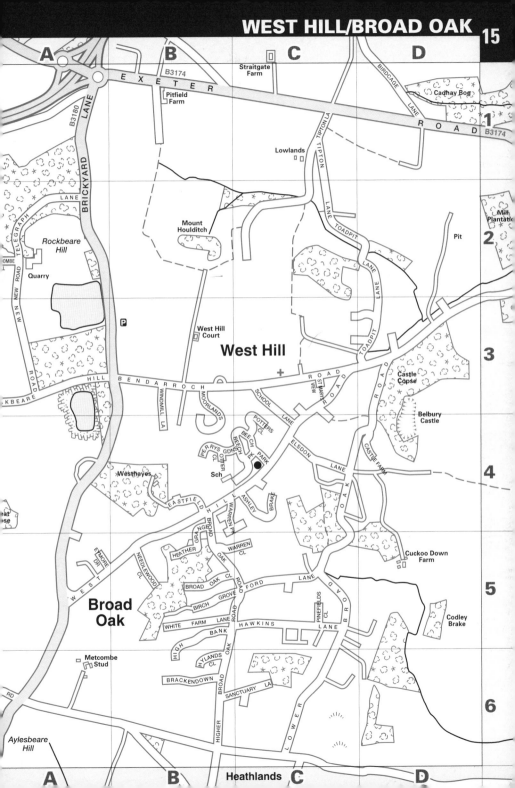

A B C D

EXETER B3174 ROAD B3174

Straitgate Farm

Pitfield Farm

Birdcage Lane

Cadhay Bog

1

BRICKYARD LANE

B3180

Lowlands

Tipton La

Tipton Lane

Mill Plantation

Pit

2

TELEGRAPH LANE

Rockbeare Hill

Quarry

Mount Houlditch

Toadpit Lane

NEW NEW ROAD

OMBE

West Hill Court

P

West Hill

West Hill Court

Toadpit Lane

Castle Copse

3

KBEARE

ROAD

HILL

BENDARROCH

WINDMILL LA

MOORLANDS

SCHOOL LANE

ST MARYS

VIEW

ROAD

ROAD

Belbury Castle

CASTLE FARM

POTTERS CL

BEECH PARK

PERRYS GDNS

OTTER

BEECH

Sch

ELSDON

ELSDON LANE

OAK

4

Westhayes

EASTFIELD

GRANGE

BROAD

HILL

WARREN PK

ASHLEY

BRAKE

Cuckoo Down Farm

HEATHER CL

WARREN CL

NEEDLEWOOD CL

ELMORE DRI

WEST

Codley Brake

5

Broad Oak

BROAD OAK CL

BIRCH

GROVE

ROAD

FORD

OAK

LANE

PINEFIELDS CL

BROAD

6

WHITE FARM LANE

BANK

HAWKINS

LANE

Metcombe Stud

HIGH

H'LANDS CL

BROAD OAK

SANCTUARY LA

HIGHER

LOWER

BRACKENDOWN

RD

Aylesbeare Hill

A B **Heathlands** C D

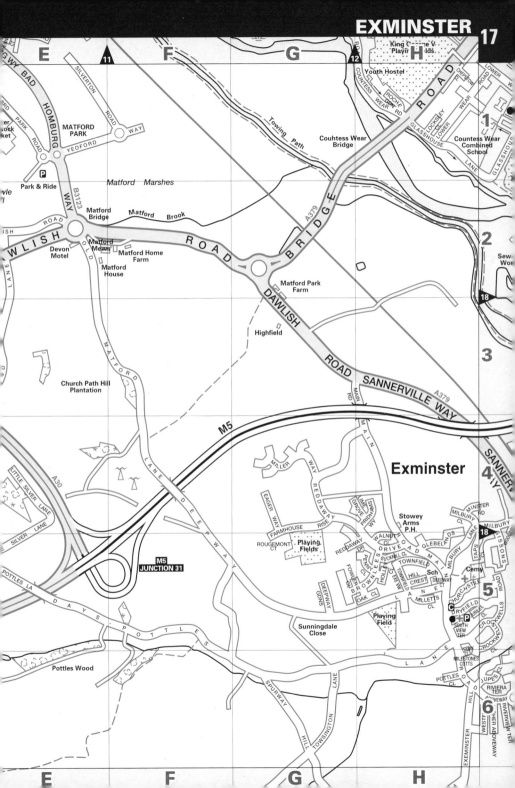

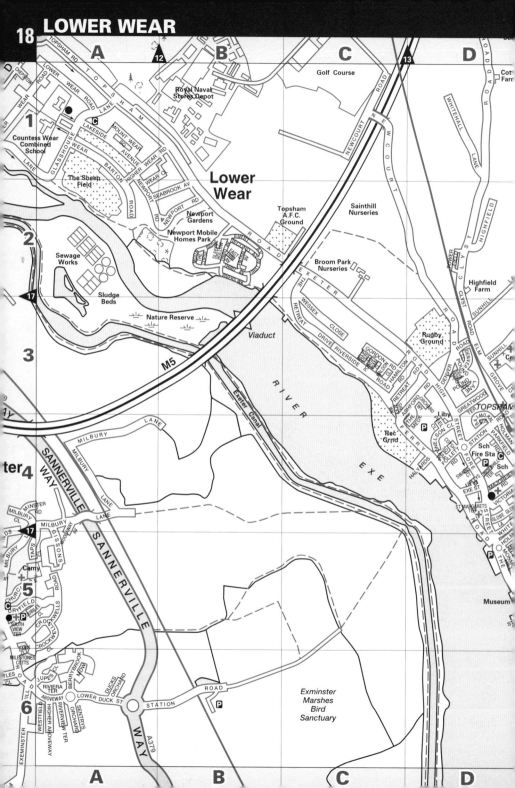

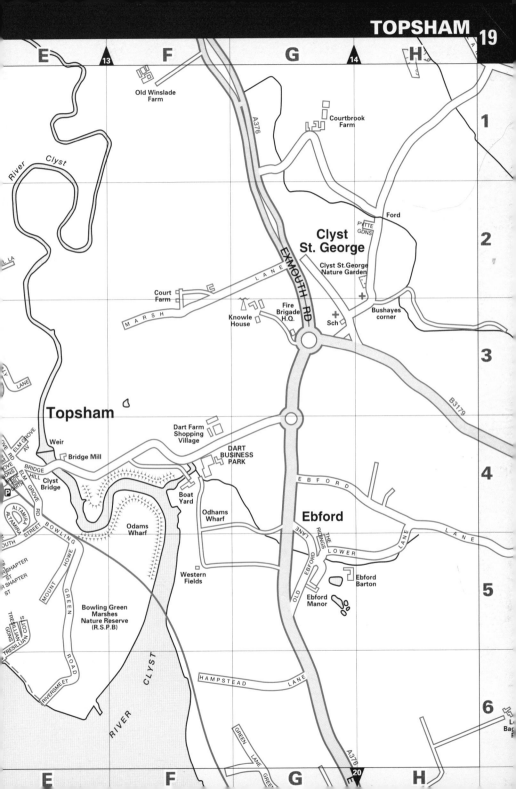

E ▲ 13 **F** **G** ▲ 14 **H**

Old Winslade Farm

Courtbrook Farm

River Clyst

1

Ford

PYTTE GDNS

Clyst St. George

2

Clyst St.George Nature Garden

Court Farm

EXMOUTH RD

MARSH LANE

Knowle House

Fire Brigade H.Q.

Sch

Bushayes corner

3

B3179

Topsham

Weir

Dart Farm Shopping Village

DART BUSINESS PARK

4

Bridge Mill

ELM GROVE AV

EBFORD

ELM GROVE RD

BRIDGE HILL

Clyst Bridge

P

Boat Yard

Odhams Wharf

Ebford

ALTAMIRA RD

ALTAMIRA

BOWLING

STREET

Odams Wharf

THE RIDINGS

OLD EBFORD LANE

LANE

LANE

LOWER

SHAPTER ST

SHAPTER ST

MOUNT HOWE

GREEN

Western Fields

Ebford Barton

5

TRESILLIAN GDNS

S.LLO

TRESILLIAN

ROAD

Bowling Green Marshes Nature Reserve (R.S.P.B)

Ebford Manor

RIVERSMEET

CLYST

HAMPSTEAD LANE

6

RIVER CLYST

GREEN LANE GREEN

A376

▲ 20

E **F** **G** **H**

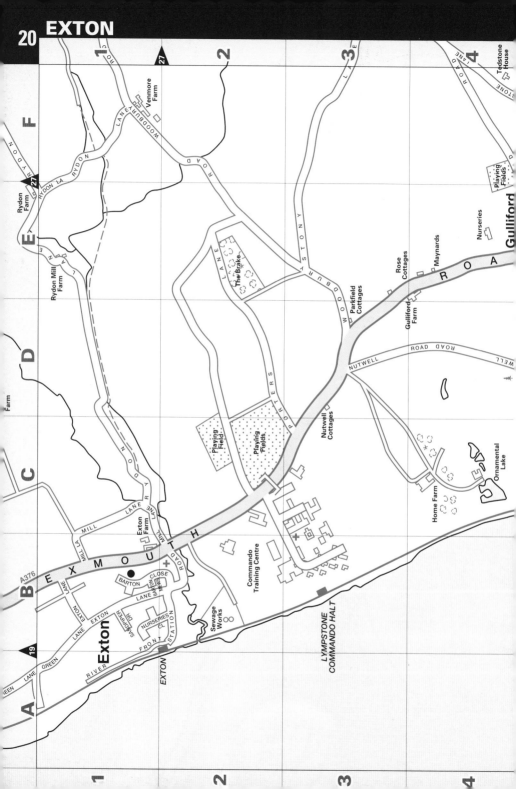

Exton

Gulliford

Tedstone House

Venmore Farm

Rydon Farm

Rydon Mill Farm

Playing Fields

Nurseries

Maynards

Rose Cottages

Parkfield Cottages

Gulliford Farm

The Brakes

Nutwell Cottages

NUTWELL ROAD

ROAD

Home Farm

Ornamental Lake

Playing Field

Playing Fields

Exton Farm

Commando Training Centre

BARTON

NURSERIES CL

Sewage Works

LYMPSTONE COMMANDO HALT

MILL LANE

EXTON LANE

GREEN LANE

RIVER FRONT

STATION ROAD

EXTON

A376

TEDSTONE LANE

Watton Bridge

Watton Brook

24

A-la-Ronda (NT)

SUMMER LA

Courtlands Cross

LITTLEMEAD

A376

SWS
APRIL RD
ELM
GRO
ASH

RIVERMEAD
LAMP CL
ELMFIELD
SYLVAN CL
RNFIELD

CREST
MOUNT

CRESCENT
FEATHER

ROAD EXETER ROAD EXE
SEAFIELD AVENUE
FEATHERBED
IONA WAY CL
LANE

F

Harefield
(St Peters School)

Potters Farm

WOTTON ROAD

Thorn Farm

XMOUTH

HILL

JUBILEE RD
MAL FIELD
MEADOW CL

Mount Pleasant

LONGBROOK

Courtlands

E

Lympstone Grange

MO HAREFIELD

STRAWBERRY GRANGE RD
BIRCH RD
LONGMEAD

STONE
LA

ORCHARD CL

NEWBURGH CRES
GLEBELANDS RD
CLETON CL
MEETHILL RD
GLEBE RD

NUTWELL
GIBRALTAR
TRAFALGAR

SCHOOL HILL
Sch

GREENHILL AV

BURNHAMS
HILL

BURGMANS

LYMPSTONE

STRAND

CHURCH HILL

UNDERHILL
UNDERHILL CL
CRES

CHAPEL ST

HIGHCLIFF

HIGHCLIFFE CT

SOWDEN

UNDERHILL

LANE SOWDEN

THE QUAY

22

D

COURTLANDS LANE

DAWLISH LANE
PK TER

Sowden Farm

Mussel Purification Station

Lympstone

Daniel's Corner

Darling's Rock

Lympstone Lake

Lympstone

C

E X E

The Ridge

RIVER EXE

B

A

5   6   7   8

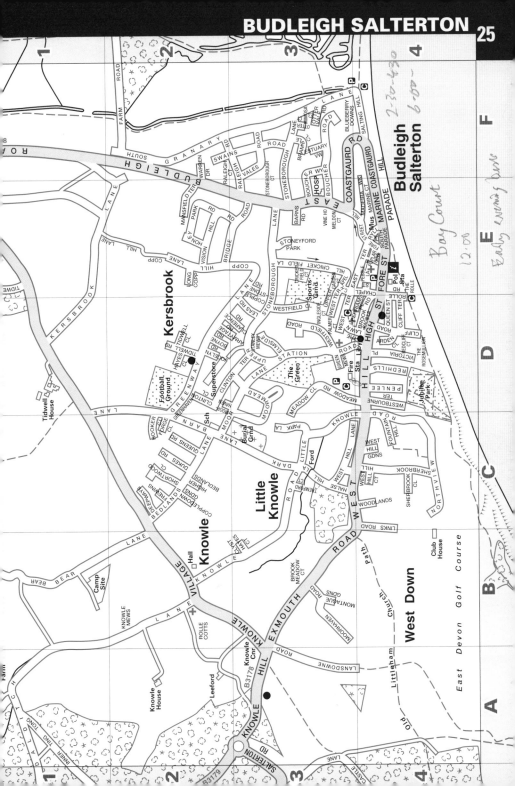

A B C D

1

Warbore
Plantation

Rifle Range

Staplake
Mount

STAPLAKE RISE

A379

THE P

STARCROSS

Starcross

COURTENAY RD

LONGFIELD ESTATE

HEYWOOD

BRICKYARD

BONHAY CL

BARLEY WK

PEACOCK PL

SERCOMBES GDNS

BONHAY RD

WELL RD

COURTENAY RD

2

Vennbridge
Farm

ROAD

COOKSONS

DREW

NEW

LANE

CHURCH

Sch

Rec
Grnd

PARKERS

SWAN RD

BRUNEL RD

WESTERN

HAMILTON

BISHOPS

ELM

STROYAL

COLTERS

CRES

P

Surgery

THE STRAND

Jetty

Passeng

Passenger Ferry
to Exmouth
(Summer Only)

STAPLAKE

LANE

ROAD

NEW

GENERALS

GENERALS
CL

COUNTESS CRES

3

Easter
Hill

Oak Meadow
Golf Club

ROAD

THE STRAND

4

Cofford
Farm

ROAD

LANE

CHURCH

WESTWOOD
HILL

MIDDLEWOOD

HILL

VICARAGE RD

COFTON HILL

COFTON HILL

DAWLISH

Sch

SCHOOL

HILL

CRES

HILL

Cockwood

5

EXETER ROAD

COFTON

Caravan
Park

Caravan
Park

WESTWOOD
HILL

COFTON

WARREN

LANE

ROAD

6

PORT

ROAD

EXETER RD

A379

ORCHARD

LANE

Eastdon

A B C D

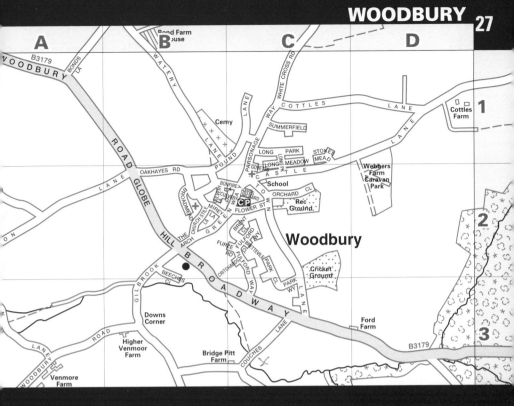

Bond Farm House
Cemy
WHITE CROSS RD
COTTLES LANE
WATERY LANE
B3179 WOODBURY
BONDS LA
ROAD LANE GLOBE HILL
OAKHAYES RD
POUND LANE
PARSONAGE LANE
CASTLE LANE
GOVERNMENT
LONG MEADOW WAY
SUMMERFIELD
LONG PARK
STOKES MEADOW
Webbers Farm Caravan Park
Cottles Farm
School
ORCHARD CL
Rec Ground
Woodbury
BONFIRE HAYES ORCHARD
BROADMEAD
THE ARCH
CHURCH STILE LA
MIREY LA
FLOWER ST
GREEN
BRENT
FURZE HILL FULFORD
FULFORD RD
BRETTEVILLE PARK
PARK WY
CRITCHMEAD
FULFORD WAY
PARK LANE
Cricket Ground
GILBROOK
BEECHES CL
Downs Corner
ROAD LANE
Higher Venmoor Farm
Bridge Pitt Farm
COUCHES LANE
Ford Farm
B3179
Venmore Farm
WOODBURY

A - Z INDEX TO STREETS
with Postcodes

Index includes some ...es for which there is insuf-
nt space on the maps.
...se names are preceded by
* and are followed by the
...est adjoining thorough-

...ROADCLYST

...nd Rd EX5 9 B2
...clyst Vw EX5 9 B2
...ch Cl EX5 9 B2
...d Vw EX5 9 B2
...ow Rd EX5 9 B1
...rch Cl EX5 9 B1
...rch La EX5 9 B1
... Cl EX5 9 B2
...cey Ct EX5 9 B1
...en Tree Rd EX5 9 C2
...ings Gdns EX5 9 B1
...y Cl EX5 9 B1
...e Cl EX5 9 B2
...ole Rd EX5 9 B2
...v Buildings EX5 9 B1
...Tree Cl EX5 9 B2
...Coach Rd EX5 9 B2
...hard Gdns EX5 9 B3
...ndsland EX5 9 B2

Queens Sq EX5 9 B1
Sanders Cl EX5 9 B2
Sandy La EX5 9 C3
School La EX5 9 B1
Small La EX5 9 B1
Station Rd EX5 9 B3
Sunnyfield EX5 9 B1
Sycamore Cl EX5 9 B2
Tower Vw EX5 9 B3
Town End EX5 9 B1
Town Hill EX5 9 B1
Willow Gdns EX5 9 B2
Wiltshier Cl EX5 9 B1
Woodbury Vw EX5 9 B3
Woodland Mews EX5 9 B2
Woodland Rd EX5 9 B2

BROAD OAK / WEST HILL

Allercombe Hill EX11 15 A2
Ashley Brake EX11 15 C4
Beech Pk EX11 15 C4
Bendarroch Rd EX11 15 B3
Birch Gro EX11 15 B5
Birdcage La EX11 15 D1
Brackendown EX11 15 B6
Brickyard La EX11 15 A2
Broad Oak Rd EX11 15 B4
Broadoak Cl EX11 15 B5
Castle Farm EX11 15 D4
Eastfield EX11 15 B4
Elsdon La EX11 15 C4

Exeter Rd EX11 15 B1
Eymore Dr EX11 15 A5
Ford La EX11 15 C5
Hawkins La EX11 15 C5
Heather Grange EX11 15 B5
High Bank EX11 15 B6
Higher Broad Oak Rd EX11 15 B6
Hylands Cl EX11 15 B6
Lower Broad Oak Rd EX11 15 C6
Moorlands EX11 15 B3
Needlewood Cl EX11 15 B5
New Rd EX11 15 A3
Oak Rd EX11 15 A6
Otter Cl EX11 15 B4
Perrys Gdns EX11 15 B4
Pinefields Cl EX11 15 C5
Potters Cl EX11 15 C4
Rockbeare Hill EX11 15 A3
St Marys Vw EX11 15 C3
Sanctuary La EX11 15 B6
School La EX11 15 C3
Telegraph La EX11 15 A2
Tipton La EX11 15 C1
Toadpit La EX11 15 C2
Warren Cl EX11 15 B5
Warren Pk EX11 15 B4
West Hill Rd EX11 15 A5
White Farm La EX11 15 B5
Windmill La EX11 15 B3

BUDLEIGH SALTERTON

Arden Cl EX9 25 D4
Armytage Rd EX9 25 D3
Barn La EX9 25 C2
Barns Rd EX9 25 E3
Bear La EX9 25 B1
Bedlands La EX9 25 C2
Blueberry Downs EX9 25 F3
Boucher Rd EX9 25 E3
Boucher Way EX9 25 E3
Boyne Rd EX9 25 D2
Bramble Cl EX9 25 F3
Bridge Rd EX9 25 E3
Brook Meadow Ct EX9 25 B3
Brook Rd EX9 25 D4
Chapel Hill EX9 25 E3
Chapel St EX9 25 D3
Clarence Rd EX9 25 D3
Cliff Rd EX9 25 D4
Cliff Ter EX9 25 D4
Clinton Cl EX9 25 D2
Clinton Ter EX9 25 D2
Clyst Hayes Ct EX9 25 B3
Coastgaurd Hill EX9 25 E4
Coastgaurd Rd EX9 25 E3
Copp Hill La EX9 25 E3
Coppledown Gdns EX9 25 C2
Copplestone Rd EX9 25 D3
Cricket Field Ct EX9 25 E3
Cricket Field La EX9 25 E3
Dalditch La EX9 25 A1
Dark La EX9 25 C3
Deepways EX9 25 C2
Dukes Rd EX9 25 C2

East Budleigh Rd EX9 25 E3
East Ter EX9 25 E4
Elmside EX9 25 D3
Estuary Vw EX9 25 F3
Exmouth Rd EX9 25 B3
Fore St EX9 25 E4
Fore St Hill EX9 25 E4
Forge Cl EX9 25 C2
Fountain Hill EX9 25 C4
Frewins EX9 25 C2
Garden Ct EX9 25 E3
Granary La EX9 25 F2
Green Mews EX9 25 D2
Greenhaven EX9 25 C2
Greenway La EX9 25 D2
Halse Hill La EX9 25 C3
Hayes Cl EX9 25 D2
High St EX9 25 D4
Higher Bedlands EX9 25 C2
Honey Park Rd EX9 25 E2
Hooker Cl EX9 25 C2
Ingleside Ct EX9 25 D3
Inner Ting Tong EX9 25 A1
Jocelyn Rd EX9 25 D2
Kersbrook La EX9 25 D1
Knowle Hill EX9 25 A3
Knowle Mews EX9 25 B2
Knowle Rd EX9 25 B2
Knowle Village EX9 25 B3
Lansdowne Rd EX9 25 A3
Leas Rd EX9 25 D3
Links Rd EX9 25 C4
Little Knowle EX9 25 C3
Long Copp EX9 25 E2

Madeira Walk EX9 25 E4
Mansfield Ter EX9 25 E2
Marine Ct EX9 25 E4
Marine Parade EX9 25 E4
Meadow Cl EX9 25 D3
Meadow Rd EX9 25 D4
Meldon Ct EX9 25 E3
Mimosa Ct EX9 25 F3
Montague Gdns EX9 25 B3
Moor La EX9 25 C2
Moorhaven EX9 25 D2
Moorhaven Rd EX9 25 B3
Moormead EX9 25 C3

Northview Rd EX9 25 C4

Otter Ct EX9 25 F3
Ottervale Rd EX9 25 F3

Palmer Ct EX9 25 D3
Park La EX9 25 C3
Pebble La EX9 25 E4
Penlee EX9 25 D4
Perriams Pl EX9 25 D3
Poplar Row EX9 25 E4

Queen St EX9 25 D4
Queens Rd EX9 25 C2

Ragg La EX9 25 D4
Raleigh Ct EX9 25 E2
Raleigh Rd EX9 25 E3
Redclffff Ct EX9 25 D4
Redhills EX9 25 D4
Rolle Cotts EX9 25 B2
Rolle Rd EX9 25 E4
Ryll La EX9 25 E4

Salting Hill EX9 25 F4
Sherbrook Cl EX9 25 C4
Sherbrook Hill EX9 25 C2
Shortwood Cl EX9 25 C2
South Farm Rd EX9 25 F2
South Parade EX9 25 E4
Stanley Mews EX9 25 D3
Station Rd EX9 25 D3
Stoneborough Ct EX9 25 E3
Stoneborough La EX9 25 E3
Stoneyford Pk EX9 25 E3
Swains Rd EX9 25 F2

The Lawn EX9 25 D4
The Rolle EX9 25 D4
The Rosemullion EX9 25 D4
Tidwell Cl EX9 25 D2
Tidwell La EX9 25 E1
Tidwell Rd EX9 25 D2
Tremford Ct EX9 25 C3

Upper Stoneborough La EX9 25 D3
Upper West Ter EX9 25 D3

Vales Rd EX9 25 F3
Victoria Pl EX9 25 D4
Vine Ho EX9 25 E3
Vision Hill Rd EX9 25 C4

Warren Dr EX9 25 F2
West Hill EX9 25 C4
West Hill Ct EX9 25 C4
West Hill Gdns EX9 25 C4
West Hill La EX9 25 C3
West Ter EX9 25 D3
Westbourne Ter EX9 25 D4
Westfield Cl EX9 25 D3
Westfield Rd EX9 25 D3
Woodlands EX9 25 C4

COCKWOOD / STARCROSS

Barley Walk EX6 26 C2
Bishops Cl EX6 26 D2
Bonhay Cl EX6 26 C1
Bonhay Rd EX6 26 D2
Brickyard La EX6 26 C2
Brunel Rd EX6 26 C2

Chapple Cl EX6 26 D2
Church Rd EX6 26 D2
Church St EX6 26 C2
Cofton Hill EX6 26 C5
Cofton La EX6 26 B5
Cookson Rd EX6 26 C2
Counties Cres EX6 26 D2
Courtenay Cl EX6 26 C1
Courtenay Ter EX6 26 D2

Dawlish Warren Rd EX6 26 D4
Drews Cl EX6 26 C2

Elm Ct EX6 26 D2

Exeter Rd EX6 26 A6

Generals Cl EX6 26 C3
Generals La EX6 26 C3

Hamilton Gro EX6 26 D3
Heywood Dr EX6 26 C1

Kenbury Cres EX6 26 D4

Longfield Est EX6 26 C1

Middlewood Hill EX6 26 C5

New Rd EX6 26 C2

Orchard La EX6 26 C6

Parkers Rd EX6 26 C2
Peacock Pl EX6 26 C2
Port Rd EX6 26 A6

Royal Way EX6 26 D2

School Hill EX6 26 D4
Sercombes Gdns EX6 26 C2
Staplake La EX6 26 B3
Staplake Rd EX6 26 C1
Staplake Rise EX6 26 C1
Swan Rd EX6 26 C2

The Strand EX6 26 C1

Vicarage Rd EX6 26 C4

Well St EX6 26 D2
Western Dr EX6 26 D2
Westwood Hill EX6 26 C4

EXETER

Abbeville Cl EX2 11 H4
Abbey Ct EX2 13 G2
Abbey Rd EX4 6 A5
Abbots Rd EX4 5 H5
Aboveway EX6 18 A6
Acland Rd EX4 5 G6
Acland Ter EX4 5 D2
Addison Cl EX4 10 C1
Alba Ct EX1 7 F6
Albert Pl EX1 3 C5
Albert St EX1 5 H6
Alberta Cres EX4 6 B4
Albion Pl EX4 5 H5
Albion St EX4 3 A5
Aldens Grn EX2 11 E6
Aldens Rd EX2 16 C1
Alderson Dr EX2 13 E1
Aldrin Rd EX4 5 H3
Alexandra Ter EX4 5 H6
Alexandra Walk EX2 13 E1
Alford Cl EX1 6 D5
Alford Cres EX1 6 C6
Alfranza Cl EX1 12 C1
Aller Vale Cl EX2 12 C2
Allhallows Ct EX4 3 B4
Allington Mead EX4 5 E2
Alma Pl EX2 12 A2
Alpha St EX1 12 A1
Alphinbrook Rd EX2 11 F6
Alphington Cross EX2 11 E5
Alphington Rd EX2 11 E5
Alphington Spur EX2 11 E6
Alphington St EX2 3 B6
Altamira EX3 19 E4
Ambassador Rd EX1 7 F6
Amity Pl EX3 18 D5
Anne Ct EX4 6 A4
Anthony Rd EX1 12 A1
Antonine Cres EX4 10 B1
Apple Farm Gro EX2 13 F4
Archibald Rd EX1 11 G1
Arena Pk EX4 6 C3
Argyll Mews EX4 5 E3
Argyll Rd EX4 5 F2
Armstrong Av EX4 5 G3
Arundel Cl EX2 16 C1
Ash Farm Cl EX1 7 G4
Ash Leigh EX2 11 E6
Ashford Rd EX3 18 C3
Ashleigh Cl EX4 10 C1
Ashleigh Mount Rd EX4 10 C1
Ashton Rd EX2 11 E4
Ashwood Rd EX2 11 E4
Aspen Cl EX2 12 D3
Athelstan Rd EX1 11 G1
Atkinson Cl EX4 6 B4
Attwills Almshouses EX4 3 A2
Attwyll Av EX2 12 B2
Austen Cl EX4 6 D5
Avalon Cl EX4 6 B4
Avocet Rd EX2 13 F1
Avondale Rd EX2 12 B2

Babblebrook Mews EX1 7 G4
Bad Homburg Way EX2 11 G6
Baddon Cl EX4 6 B3
Bagshot Av EX2 11 H3
Bailey St EX4 3 D3
Baker St EX2 12 A1
Bakers Hill EX2 10 A4
Balls Farm Rd EX2 10 C5
Balmoral Gdns EX3 18 D4
Bampfylde St EX1 3 D3
Barbican Ct EX4 3 B5
Barbican Steps EX4 3 B4
Baring Cres EX1 11 H1
Baring Ter EX2 11 G3
Barley Farm Rd EX4 10 B2
Barley La EX4 4 B6
Barley Mount EX4 10 C2
Barnardo Rd EX2 11 G2
Barnfield Cres EX1 3 D4
Barnfield Hill EX1 11 G1
Barnfield Rd EX1 3 D4
Barnstone Ct EX2 16 B1
Barrack La EX2 16 B3
Barrack Rd EX2 12 A1
Bartholomew St East EX4 3 B4
Bartholomew St West EX4 3 B5
Bartholomew Ter EX4 3 B5
Barton Cl EX3 20 B1
Barton Cl EX1 6 D6
Barton La EX2 16 A3
Barton Mews EX3 20 B1
Barton Rd EX2 10 D3
Baxter Cl EX2 13 E3
Bazley Sq EX1 7 F4
Beacon Av EX4 6 B5
Beacon Heath EX4 6 C3
Beacon La EX4 6 B5
Bear St EX1 3 C5
Beaufort Ho EX4 3 D3
Beaufort Rd EX2 3 B6
Beaworthy EX2 11 E4
Bedford St EX1 3 D4
Beech Av EX4 5 G4
Belgrave Rd EX1 5 G6
Bell Ct EX4 3 B4
Belle Vue Rd EX4 5 F2
Belmont Rd EX1 5 G6
Belvedere Cl EX3 18 C3
Belvidere Rd EX4 5 E3
Bennett Sq EX4 6 B5
Bennetts Cl EX2 11 E6
Berkshire Dr EX4 10 C2
Bernadette Cl EX4 6 D4
Berry Ct EX2 11 G2
Berrybrook Mdw EX6 18 A6
Betony Rise EX2 12 D3
Bettysmead EX4 6 B4
Bettysmead Ct EX4 6 B4
Beverley Cl EX2 12 C2
Bicton Pl EX1 12 A1
Bindon Rd EX4 7 F2
Binford Cl EX1 6 C6
Birchy Barton Hill EX1 12 C2
Birkett Cl EX2 12 D3
Bishop Westall Rd EX2 12 B3
Bishops Court Rd EX5 13 H4
Bittern Rd EX2 13 F1
Black Hat La EX6 10 A3
Blackall Rd EX4 3 C2
Blackboy Rd EX4 5 H6
Blackhorse La EX1 7 G5
Blackmore Mews EX2 12 D3
Blackthorn Cres EX1 12 D1
Blenheim Cl EX2 11 G6
Blenheim Rd EX2 11 E5
Bluecoat La EX1 3 D4
Bodley Cl EX1 6 C6
Bonhay Rd EX4 3 A2
Bonnington Gro EX1 12 A1
Bonville Cl EX1 6 C6
Bourn Rise EX4 7 E3
Bovemoors La EX2 12 A2
Bowe Ct EX1 5 H6
Bowhay La EX4 10 C2
Bowling Green Rd EX3 19 E4
Bowring Cl EX1 6 C6
Bradfield Rd EX4 7 E3
Bradman Way EX2 11 F5
Bradninch Pl EX4 3 C3
Bramley Av EX1 12 D1
Branscombe Cl EX4 10 B2
Brentor Cl EX4 4 C5
Briar Cres EX2 12 A4
Bridespring Rd EX4 6 A4
Bridespring Walk EX4 6 A4
Bridford Rd EX2 11 F4
Bridge Cotts EX4 5 G5
Bridge Ct EX4 3 B4
Bridge Hill EX3 19 E4
Bridge Rd EX2 17 G2
Bridgehill Garth EX3 19 E4
Brittany Ho EX4 3 D3
Britten Dr EX2 12 C1
Broadfield Rd EX2 12 D2

Broadgate EX1 3 C4
Broadleaf Cl EX1 7 F4
Broadmeadow Av EX4 10 D3
Broadparks Av EX4 7 F3
Broadparks Cl EX4 7 F3
Broadwalk Ho EX1 3 D4
Broadway EX2 10 C4
Brodick Cl EX4 5 H4
Brook Cl EX1 6 D5
Brook Green Ter EX4 5 G5
Brookdale EX2 12 C2
Brooke Av EX2 12 A4
Brookfield Gdns EX2 11 E6
Brookleigh Av EX1 12 C2
Brookside Cres EX4 6 C3
Brookway EX1 6 D5
Broom Cl EX2 12 B2
Browning Cl EX2 12 B3
Brownlees EX6 17 G5
Brunel Cl EX4 3 A2
Brunswick St EX4 3 A6
Buckerell Av EX2 11 H3
Buckleigh Cl EX4 7 E3
Bucknill Cl EX6 17 H5
Buddle La EX4 10 D4
Bude St EX1 3 D3
Budlake Rd EX2 11 F6
Bull Meadow Rd EX2 3 D5
Buller Rd EX4 3 A6
Bungalow La EX2 11 G3
Burnet Cl EX2 12 D4
Burns Av EX2 12 A3
Burnthouse La EX2 12 A4
Burrator Dr EX4 4 C5
Butts Ct EX2 12 B2
Butts Rd EX2 12 B2
Byron Rd EX2 13 E2
Bystock Cl EX4 3 B3
Bystock Ter EX4 3 B3

California Cl EX4 5 G2
Calthorpe Rd EX4 6 B4
Cambridge St EX4 3 A5
Camelot Cl EX4 6 B4
Campion Gdns EX2 12 C3
Canal Banks EX2 11 G4
Canberra Cl EX4 5 H2
Canon Way EX2 16 C1
Canterbury Rd EX4 4 C6
Carders Ct EX2 3 B6
Carfax EX1 3 C4
Carlile Rd EX2 12 B2
Carlton Rd EX2 12 C3
Carlyon Cl EX1 6 B6
Carlyon Gdns EX1 6 B6
Carpenter Cl EX4 3 B4
Castle Mount EX4 3 C2
Castle St EX4 3 C3
Cathedral Cl EX1 3 C4
Cathedral Yard EX1 3 C4
Catherine St EX1 3 C4
Causey Gdns EX1 7 F3
Causey La EX1 7 F3
Cavendish Rd EX1 12 A1
Cecil Rd EX2 3 A6
Cedars Rd EX2 3 D6
Celia Cres EX4 6 B2
Cemetery Pl EX4 3 B4
Central Av, Exeter EX4 6 C3
Central Av, Newport Pk EX2 18 B2
Chamberlain Rd EX2 11 F3
Chancel Cl EX4 7 E3
Chancel La EX4 7 E3
Chancellors Way EX4 6 B2
Chandlers Walk EX2 11 F3
Chanter Cl EX2 12 B5
Chantry Mdw EX2 16 C1
Chapel Rd EX2 11 E6
Chapel St EX1 3 D4
Chard Rd EX1 12 B1
Chardstock Cl EX1 13 E1
Charingthay Gate EX4 5 H4
Charnley Av EX4 10 C2
Chaucer Av EX2 12 A4
Cheeke St EX1 5 G6
Chelmsford Rd EX4 4 B6
Cheltenham Cl EX4 4 B6
Chepstow Cl EX2 17 H1
Cherry Gdns EX2 12 B2
Cherry Tree Cl EX4 5 E2
Chester Cl EX4 4 C6
Chestnut Av EX2 12 B3
Chestnut Ct EX2 11 F6
Cheyne Rise EX4 7 E3
Cheyneagate La EX4 6 D1
Chichester Ho EX2 12 C2
Chichester Mews EX1 3 D4
Christow Rd EX2 11 F4
Chudleigh Rd EX2 11 F6
Church Hill EX4 6 D1
Church La, Clyst St Mary EX5 14 A4
Church La, Exeter EX2 13 D3
Church La, Heavitree EX2 12 A2

Church La, Pinhoe EX4
Church Path EX2 7 F4
Church Path Rd EX2
Church Rd, Alphington EX2
Church Rd, Exeter EX2
Church Rd, St Thomas EX2
Church Side EX5
Church St EX2
Church Stile EX6
Church Ter EX2
Churchill Rd EX2
Chute St EX1
City Arcade EX4
Clapperbrook La EX2
Clara Pl EX3
Claremont Gro EX2 12 B3
Clarence Pl EX4
Clarence Rd EX4
Clarke Mead EX2
Clayton Rd EX4
Cleve Rd EX4
Clevedon Cl EX4
Cleveland Ct EX1
Cleveland St EX4
Cliff Bastin Cl EX2 11 F6
Clifford Cl EX1
Clifford Rd EX4
Clifton Cotts EX1
Clifton La EX2
Clifton Rd EX1
Clifton St EX1
Clinton Av EX4
Clinton St EX4
Clipper Quay EX2
Cloister Rd EX4
Cludens Cl EX2
Clydesdale Rd EX4
Clyst Halt Av EX2
Clyst Heath EX2
Clyst Rd EX3
Clyst St Mary By-Pass
Clyst Valley Rd EX5
Coates Rd EX2
Codrington St EX1
Cofton Rd EX2
Colands Ct EX2
Coleridge Rd EX2
College Av EX1
College La EX1
College Rd EX1
Colleton Cres EX2
Colleton Gro EX2
Colleton Hill EX2
Colleton Mews EX2
Colleton Row EX2
Collins Rd EX2
Commercial Rd EX2
Commercial Rd EX1
Commins Rd EX1
Coney Ct EX2
Coneybeare EX1
Conrad Av EX4
Coombe St EX1
Copplestone Dr EX4
Cordery Rd EX2
Cornflower Hill EX4
Cornmill Cres EX2
Cornwall St EX4
Coronation Rd EX2
Cotfield St EX2
Cotterell Rd EX5
Cottey Cres EX4
Countess Wear Rd EX2
Couper Mdws EX2
Courtenay Gdns EX2
Courtenay Rd EX2
Coventry Rd EX4
Coverdale Rd EX2
Cowick Hill EX2
Cowick La EX2
Cowick Rd EX2
Cowick St EX4
Cowley Bridge Rd EX4
Cowley Mede EX4
Cowley Vw EX4
Cowper Av EX2
Coysh Sq EX3
Crabb La EX2
Cranbrook Rd EX2
Cranmere Ct EX2
Crawford Gdns EX1
Creadly La EX3
Crediton Rd EX4
Creely Cl EX2
Cricklepit St EX1
Crockwells Cl EX6
Crockwells Rd EX6
Croft Chase EX4
Cross View EX2
Cross View Ter EX2
Culverland Cl EX4
Culverland Rd EX4
Curlew Way EX4
Cygnet EX2

et Ct EX2 11 G3
ess Dr EX4 4 C6

/ Cl EX6 17 H6
/ Links EX4 4 B5
side Rd EX4 5 H4
y La EX4 7 E2
s Rd EX4 3 C1
sway EX4 7 F3
in Ct EX2 3 D6
ish Rd EX2 11 F6
n Cl EX1 6 B6
-Pottles La EX6 16 C5
a Rue Way EX4 7 E3
on Cl EX2 16 C1
St EX2 3 D5
ery Pl EX1 3 C4
dene Pk EX2 11 H3
way Ct EX6 17 H5
way Gdns EX6 17 G5
way La EX6 17 F4
s Cres EX2 12 D2
se Cl EX2 11 E6
nark Rd EX1 11 G1
er Cl EX3 18 D3
er Rd EX3 18 D3
n Rd EX4 6 A5
nshire Pl EX4 5 G5
ond Rd EX2 3 C6
Pym Cl EX2 12 D2
ns Dr EX2 12 A4
y Dr EX2 13 E4
am Cres EX4 3 B4
am Mews EX4 3 B4
am Rd EX4 3 B4
Field EX1 3 D4
ors Walk EX2 10 B4
am Cl EX4 5 G3
et Av EX4 10 C3
n Cl EX1 13 E1
Way EX2 10 B4
e Av EX2 13 E1
es Farm EX2 10 B5
es Rd EX4 3 A6
cott Cl EX2 12 B3
en Rd EX2 12 A3
eld EX6 17 H5
s Orch EX6 18 A6
worth Rd EX2 10 D3
hideock Rd EX2 10 B6
ich Cl EX2 11 H2
ford Gdns EX4 10 C3
ford Rd EX2 10 B4
egan Cl EX4 4 D4
am Cl EX1 6 D6
n Ct EX3 18 D5
s Ct EX2 3 B6

r Way EX6 17 G4
e Cotts EX4 3 A5
e Way EX2 13 G2
es Nest EX2 10 B3
Richards Rd North
2 11 H4
Richards Rd South
2 12 A4
Av EX1 6 A6
Grove Rd EX2 11 G2
John Walk EX1 5 H6
View Ter EX4 5 G5
Wonford Hill EX2 12 B2
ern Av EX2 18 B2
gate EX1 3 D3
n Dr EX1 11 G1
d La EX3 19 G4
gton Rd EX2 11 E3
aston Mead EX2 12 D3
rton Park Rd EX4 3 D1
burgh Dr EX4 4 C6
onton Cl EX4 6 B4
und St EX2 3 B5
n Rd EX2 11 E3
m Av EX2 11 H3
e Cl EX4 6 B3
rtree Gdns EX4 3 A2
Cl EX2 12 D2
beth Av EX4 5 H4
ds Cl EX2 12 A4
Way EX2 13 E2
t Cl EX4 5 H3
Gro Rd EX3 18 D3
Grove Av EX3 19 E4
Grove Gdns EX3 19 E4
Grove Rd,
eter EX4 3 B2
Grove Rd,
psham EX3 18 D3
ridge Gdns EX4 5 E4
ton Cl EX4 5 G4
ide EX4 5 H5
ide Cl EX4 5 H5
Rd EX4 6 A5
l EX4 4 B6
anuel Cl EX4 3 A5
anuel Rd EX4 3 A5
eror Way EX1 7 F6

Endfield Cl EX1 12 C1
Endsleigh Cres EX5 8 A5
Ennerdale Way EX4 4 D6
Essex Cl EX4 10 C3
Etonhurst Cl EX2 13 E4
Ewings Sq EX2 3 C5
Exbridge Ho EX2 3 B5
Excalibur Cl EX4 6 C4
Exe Bridge North EX2 3 B6
Exe Bridge South EX2 3 B6
Exe St, Exeter EX4 3 B4
Exe St, Topsham EX3 18 D4
Exe Vale Rd EX2 12 B5
Exe Valley Way EX4 4 D6
Exe View EX6 17 H5
Exe View Cotts EX4 4 D5
Exeminster Hill EX6 17 H6
Exeter Rd EX3 18 C2
Exhibition Way EX4 7 E4
Exmouth Rd,
Clyst St Mary EX5 13 H5
Exmouth Rd,
Exton EX3 20 B1
Exonia Pk EX2 10 B3
Exton La EX3 20 B1
Exton Rd EX2 11 F4
Exwick Ct EX4 4 D5
Exwick Hill EX4 4 C5
Exwick La EX4 4 A6
Exwick Rd EX4 4 D6
Exwick Villas EX4 4 D6

Fair Oak Cl EX6 9 B3
Fairfax Gdns EX2 11 E5
Fairfield Av EX4 6 D5
Fairfield Rd EX2 16 C1
Fairfield Ter EX2 11 E3
Fairhazel Dr EX4 4 C6
Fairmead Ct EX1 7 F4
Fairpark Cl EX2 11 G2
Fairpark Rd EX2 3 D5
Fairview Av EX5 14 C4
Fairview Ter EX1 7 G4
Falcon Rd EX2 13 F3
Falkland Cl EX4 5 H2
Farleys Ct EX3 18 D4
Farm Cl EX2 12 D2
Farm Hill EX4 4 B5
Farmhouse Av EX1 7 F4
Farmhouse Rise EX6 17 G5
Feltrim Av EX2 11 G3
Ferndale Gdns EX2 11 E3
Ferndale Rd EX2 11 E3
Fernpark Cl EX2 12 A4
Ferry Rd EX3 18 C4
Filmer Way EX2 11 F4
Fingle Cl EX4 4 C5
Firs Pk EX2 10 A4
First Av, Exeter EX1 6 A6
First Av,
Newport Park EX2 18 B2
Flayes Almshouses EX4 6 D5
Florida Dr EX4 5 G2
Flowerpot La EX4 3 A5
Follett Rd EX3 18 D4
Fordland Bottom Rd
EX2 10 A6
Fords Rd EX2 11 F3
Fore St Centre EX4 3 B5
Fore St, Exeter EX4 3 B5
Fore St, Heavitree EX1 12 A1
Fore St, Ide EX2 10 B5
Fore St, Topsham EX3 18 D4
Fortescue Rd EX2 11 E4
Foundry Ct EX2 3 C6
Fouracre Cl EX4 6 B4
Fowey Cl EX1 6 A5
Fowler Cl EX6 17 G5
Fox Rd EX4 6 C3
Foxglove Rise EX4 4 B5
Foxhayes Rd EX4 4 D6
Foxtor Rd EX4 4 B5
Francis Cl EX4 10 D3
Franklin St EX2 3 D6
Franklyn Cl EX2 10 D4
Franklyn Dr EX2 10 D3
Friars Gate EX2 3 C5
Friars Walk EX2 3 D5
Friernhay St EX4 3 B4
Frog La EX5 13 H4
Frog St EX1 3 B5
Fulford Rd EX1 6 B5
Fullers Ct EX2 3 B6

Gabriel Ct EX2 3 C6
Gabriel Ho EX1 3 C5
Gabriels Wharf EX2 11 G4
Galahad Cl EX4 6 B3
Galmpton Rise EX4 6 A3
Gandy St EX4 3 C3
Garden Cl EX2 12 D3
Gareth Cres EX4 6 B3
Garland Cl EX4 4 B4
Gater La EX1 3 C5
Geneva Cl EX2 12 A3
George St EX1 3 C4

Georges Cl EX1 6 C6
Gervase Av EX2 3 B6
Gilbert Av EX2 12 D3
Gipsy Hill La EX1 7 F5
Gipsy Hill Mews EX1 7 G5
Gipsy La EX1 7 G5
Gissons EX6 18 A5
Gittisham Cl EX1 13 E1
Gladstone Rd EX1 11 H1
Glasshouse La EX2 17 H1
Glastonbury Cl EX4 6 B3
Glave Saunders Av EX2 12 D3
Glebelands EX6 17 H5
Glen Cl EX5 14 C4
Glen Walk EX4 5 H3
Glenmore Rd EX2 12 B2
Glenthorne Rd EX4 4 D3
Glenwood Rise EX2 11 G3
Globe La EX3 18 D4
Globefields EX3 18 D4
Gloucester Rd EX4 4 B6
Goldsmith St,
Exeter EX4 3 C4
Goldsmith St,
Heavitree EX1 12 A1
Good Shepherd Dr EX2 3 D5
Gordon Rd, Exeter EX1 5 H6
Gordon Rd,
Topsham EX3 18 C3
Gordons Pl EX2 12 B2
Grace Rd EX2 11 F5
Grafton Rd EX4 4 D4
Grainger Cl EX2 12 D2
Grandisson Ct EX2 12 B5
Grasslands Dr EX1 7 F4
Great Hill Vw EX4 5 H2
Greatwood Ter EX3 18 D3
Grecian Way EX2 12 D3
Green La, Exeter EX4 10 C2
Green La, Exton EX3 19 G6
Greenacres EX4 4 D2
Greenford Villas EX2 11 F3
Greenpark Av EX1 7 E6
Greenway EX2 10 C3
Greenwood Dr EX2 13 E2
Grenadier Rd EX1 7 F6
Grendon Rd EX1 11 H1
Grenville Av EX4 7 E4
Grindle Way EX5 14 A5
Grosvenor Pl EX1 5 H6
Grove Hill EX3 19 E3
Guildford Cl EX4 4 B6
Guinea St EX1 3 C5
Guinevere Way EX4 6 B4
Guinness La EX4 4 C5
Guys Rd EX4 10 D1

Haccombe Cl EX4 10 C1
Hadrian Dr EX4 10 B1
Haldon Cl EX3 18 C3
Haldon Rd EX4 3 B3
Haldon View Ter EX2 12 A2
Halses Cl EX4 4 B5
Halyards EX3 18 D4
Hambeer La EX2 10 C4
Hamilton Av EX2 12 A4
Hamilton Dr EX2 13 E2
Hamilton Rd EX3 18 C3
Hamlin Gdns EX1 6 B6
Hamlin La EX1 6 B5
Hamlyns La EX4 4 C4
Hammond Croft Way
EX2 16 C1
Hampden Pl EX2 3 B6
Hampshire Cl EX4 10 C3
Hampstead La EX3 19 F6
Hampton Bldgs EX4 5 H5
Hanover Cl EX1 12 A1
Hanover Ct EX2 16 D1
Hanover Rd EX1 6 A6
Hardy Rd EX2 13 E2
Harebell Copse EX4 4 B5
Harefield Cl EX4 3 A1
Harefield Rd EX8 20 E4
Harrier Way EX2 13 F3
Harringcourt Rd EX4 7 F3
Harrington Dr EX4 7 F3
Harrington Gdns EX4 7 F3
Harrington La EX4 6 D3
Harts Cl EX1 7 F4
Harts La EX1 7 E5
Hatherleigh Rd EX2 11 E5
Haven Cl EX2 11 F3
Haven Rd EX2 3 B6
Hawthorn Rd EX2 12 A4
Hawthorn Way EX2 11 E6
Hayes Barton Ct EX4 3 A5
Hayne Cl EX4 6 C5
Haytor Dr EX4 4 C5
Hazel Rd EX2 12 B5
Hazelmead Rd EX5 14 C5
Headingley Cl EX2 12 D3
Headland Cl EX1 6 D6
Headland Cres EX1 6 D6
Headon Gdns EX2 12 B6
Heath Barton EX4 6 D3

Heath Brook Mews EX4 6 D3
Heath Rd EX2 12 C2
Heather Cl EX1 6 C6
Heavitree Pk EX1 12 B2
Heavitree Rd EX1 11 G1
Hele Rd EX4 3 A2
Hellings Park La EX5 8 C1
Hennock Ct EX2 11 G6
Hennock Rd EX2 11 G5
Hensleigh Dr EX2 11 H2
Herbert Rd EX1 6 A5
Hereford Rd EX4 4 B6
Heron EX2 13 F2
Heron Rd,
Exonia Pk EX2 10 B3
Heron Rd,
Sowton Ind Est EX2 13 F1
Herschell Rd EX4 5 H5
Hexworthy Av EX4 4 B5
High Cft EX4 5 E3
High Mdws EX4 10 C2
High St, Exeter EX4 3 C4
High St, Ide EX2 10 B6
High St, Topsham EX3 18 D3
Highcross Rd EX4 3 D1
Higher Aboveway EX6 18 A6
Higher Barley Mount
EX4 10 C1
Higher Hoopern La EX4 5 G3
Higher Kings Av EX4 5 G4
Higher Shapter Cl EX3 19 E5
Higher Shapter St EX3 19 E5
Higher Summerlands
EX1 11 H1
Higher Wear Rd EX2 18 A2
Highfield EX3 18 D2
Hill Barton Cl EX1 6 D5
Hill Barton La EX1 6 D6
Hill Barton Rd EX1 6 D6
Hill Cl EX4 5 G4
Hill Crest EX6 17 H5
Hill La EX1 6 C5
Hill Rise EX1 6 D5
Hillcrest Pk EX4 5 F3
Hillsborough Av EX4 3 D1
Hillside Av EX4 3 D1
Hillyfield Rd EX1 6 D6
Hoker Rd EX2 12 B2
Holland Rd EX2 10 D3
Holley Cl EX6 17 H5
Hollow La EX1 7 E5
Holloway St EX2 3 D5
Hollowpits Ct EX2 16 C1
Holly Rd EX2 12 A4
Holman Way EX3 18 D4
Holne Ct EX4 4 C5
Holne Rise EX2 12 C2
Homefield Rd EX1 12 A1
Honey La EX1 7 G3
Honeylands Dr EX4 6 B5
Honeylands Way EX4 6 B5
Honeysuckle Ct EX4 4 B5
Honiton Rd,
Clyst Honiton EX5 8 A5
Honiton Rd, Exeter EX1 12 C2
Hoopern Av EX4 5 G4
Hoopern La EX4 3 D1
Hoopern St EX4 3 C1
Hope Pl EX2 12 B2
Hope Rd EX2 12 B2
Hospital La EX1 7 E5
Howard Cl EX4 4 C5
Howell Rd EX4 3 A2
Hummingbird Cl EX1 7 F4
Hurst Av EX2 12 C2
Hutchings Mead EX1 7 G4

Iddesleigh Rd EX4 5 H5
Ide La EX2 10 B4
Ide La EX2 10 D6
Ilex Cl, Exeter EX4 6 C3
Ilex Cl, Shillingford St George
EX2 16 A5
Imperial St EX4 10 C2

INDUSTRIAL & RETAIL:
Bishops Ct Quarry Trading
Est EX2 13 F3
Bittern Industrial Units
EX2 13 F1
Chelsea Trading Est
EX2 13 E1
City Industrial Est EX2 3 C6
Dart Business Pk EX3 19 F4
Dart Farm Shopping Village
EX3 19 F4
Exebridges Retail Pk
EX4 3 B6
Exeter Airport Business Pk
EX6 9 B3
Guildhall Shopping Centre
EX4 3 C4
Harlequins Shopping Centre
EX4 3 C3
Heron Industrial Units
EX2 13 F2
Hungry Fox Est EX5 8 D2
Marsh Barton Trading Est
EX2 11 F5
Matford Business Pk
EX2 11 F6
Matford Pk EX2 17 E1
Merlin Business Pk EX6 9 B3
Park Five Business Centre
EX2 13 F3
Pinhoe Trading Est EX4 7 E4
Sandpiper Ct Trading Est
EX4 7 E3
Sowton Industrial Est
EX2 13 F2
Stone La Retail Pk EX2 11 E4
Swan Units EX2 13 F2
The Exeter Business Pk
EX1 7 F6

Iolanthe Dr EX4 6 B3
Iris Av EX2 11 E3
Iron Bridge EX4 3 B3
Isca Rd EX2 3 B6
Isleworth Rd EX4 10 C2
Iveagh Ct EX4 4 C5
Ivy Cl EX2 12 C3

James Ct EX1 11 F2
Jardine Pk EX2 11 F5
Jennifer Cl EX2 11 H3
Jesmond Rd EX1 5 H6
Jesmond Villas EX1 5 H6
John Levers Way EX4 10 D1
John St EX1 3 C5
Jubilee Cl EX6 17 H5
Jubilee Rd EX1 6 A5
Juniper Cl EX4 6 C3
Jupes Cl EX6 18 A6

Kalendarhay EX1 11 F1
Kalendarhay La EX1 3 C4
Kenbury Dr EX2 16 D1
Kendall Cl EX4 5 H6
Kennerley Av EX4 6 C5
Kennford Rd EX2 11 F4
Kent Cl EX2 12 B2
Kerswill Rd EX4 10 C3
Kestor Dr EX4 4 B5
Kestrel Way EX2 13 F2
Kilbarran Rise EX4 5 E5
Kimberley Rd EX2 3 D5
King Arthurs Rd EX4 6 B3
King Edward St EX4 4 D4
King Henrys Rd EX2 12 A4
King St EX1 3 B5
King Stephen Cl EX4 3 C1
King William St EX4 3 D3
Kingdom Mews EX4 3 A2
Kingfisher Av EX2 10 B3
Kingfisher Ct EX4 7 E4
Kingfisher Dr EX4 5 G3
Kingfisher Way EX2 13 F1
Kings Rd EX4 6 A5
Kings Wharf EX2 3 C6
Kingsgate EX4 5 G5
Kingsley Av EX4 6 C4
Kingsway EX2 12 A2
Kingswood Cl EX4 4 C5
Kinnerton Ct EX4 4 C5
Kinnerton Way EX4 4 B5
Kipling Dr EX2 12 B3
Knightley Rd EX2 11 H4
Knights Cres EX2 13 E3
Knowle Dr EX4 4 C6

Laburnum Rd EX2 12 A4
Lackaborough Ct EX2 16 B1
Ladysmith Rd EX1 6 A6
Lakelands Dr EX4 10 D1
Lakeside Av EX2 18 A1
Lamacraft Dr EX4 6 B5
Lancaster Cl EX2 12 C2
Lancelot Rd EX4 6 B3
Landhayes Rd EX4 10 D1
Lands Rd EX4 7 E3
Landscore Rd EX4 10 D2
Langaton Gdns EX1 7 G4
Langaton La EX1 7 F3
Lansdowne EX2 12 C3
Lansdowne Ter EX2 3 D6
Larch Rd EX2 10 D4
Lark Cl EX4 5 G3
Larkbeare Rd EX2 3 D6
Latimer Rd EX4 6 B4
Laurel Rd EX2 12 A4
Lawrence Av EX4 10 D2
Lawrence Cres EX1 13 E1
Laxton Av EX1 12 D1
Lebanon Cl EX4 5 H4
Legion Way EX2 11 E5
Leighdene Cl EX2 11 H3
Leighton Ter EX4 3 D2
Lethbridge Rd EX2 12 C2
Lewis Cres EX2 13 E4
Leypark Cl EX1 6 D6
Leypark Cres EX1 6 D6

Leypark Rd EX1 6 D6
Lichfield Rd EX4 4 B6
Lichgate Rd EX2 16 C1
Liffey Rise EX4 4 C5
Lilac Rd EX2 12 B4
Lily Mount EX4 4 B5
Lime Gro EX6 17 H4
Lime Kiln La EX2 12 B6
Lime Tree Cl EX2 12 D4
Limegrove Rd EX4 10 D2
Lincoln Rd EX4 4 C6
Linda Cl EX1 12 D1
Linden Vale EX4 3 B2
Linfield Gdns EX4 10 D2
Linnet Cl EX1 5 H2
Lisa Cl EX2 12 B4
Little Castle St EX4 3 D3
Little Johns Cross Hill EX2 10 C4
Little Queen St EX4 3 C4
Little Rack St EX1 3 C5
Little Silver EX4 3 B2
Little Silver La EX2 17 E4
Littleway EX2 10 C3
Livery Dole Almhouses EX1 12 A1
Lloyds Cres EX1 6 D5
Lloyds Ct EX1 6 D5
Locarno Rd EX4 10 C2
Locksley Cl EX2 17 H1
Lodge Hill EX4 5 E5
London Inn Sq EX4 3 D3
Longacres EX2 11 H2
Longbrook St EX4 3 D3
Longbrook Ter EX4 3 D3
Longdown Rd EX6 10 A4
Longmeadow EX5 13 H4
Lonsdale Rd EX1 12 C1
Looe Rd EX4 3 A2
Loram Way EX2 16 D1
Lords Way EX2 12 D3
Lovelace Gdns EX2 16 C1
Lower Albert St EX1 5 H6
Lower Argyll Rd EX4 4 D3
Lower Av EX1 6 A6
Lower Coombe St EX1 3 C5
Lower Duck St EX6 18 A6
Lower Harrington La EX4 7 F4
Lower Hill Barton Rd EX1 12 D1
Lower Kings Av EX4 5 G4
Lower La EX3 19 G5
Lower North St EX4 3 B3
Lower Shapter St EX3 19 E5
Lower St Germans Rd EX4 3 D1
Lower Summerlands EX1 11 H1
Lower Wear Rd EX2 17 H1
Lucas Av EX4 5 H5
Lucky La EX2 3 C5
Ludwell La EX2 12 B3
Lustleigh Cl EX2 12 B3
Lymeborne Av EX1 12 B1
Lyncombe Cl EX4 5 H4
Lyndhurst Rd EX2 11 H2
Lynwood Av EX4 3 A5

Maddocks Row EX4 3 C4
Madison Av EX1 6 C6
Magdalen Cotts EX1 11 G1
Magdalen Gdns EX1 11 H2
Magdalen Rd EX2 11 G2
Magdalen St EX2 3 D5
Magnolia Av EX2 12 B3
Magpie Cres EX2 10 B3
Main Rd, Exminster EX6 17 G3
Main Rd, Pinhoe EX4 7 F4
Majorfield Rd EX3 18 D4
Mallard Rd EX2 13 F2
Mallison Cl EX4 4 C5
Malvern Gdns EX2 12 B3
Mamhead Rd EX2 12 D3
Manaton Cl EX2 16 D1
Manaton Ct EX2 16 D1
Mandrake Cl EX2 11 E5
Mandrake Rd EX2 11 E6
Manor Pk EX5 13 H4
Mansfield Rd EX4 5 H5
Manston Rd EX1 6 A6
Manston Ter EX2 12 A1
Manstree Rd EX2 16 A4
Maple Rd EX2 10 D2
Mardon Hill EX4 5 E4
Margaret Rd EX4 6 A4
Maritime Ct EX2 11 F3
Market St EX1 3 C4
Markham La EX2 16 A1
Markham La EX2 16 C2
Marlborough Ct, Lyndurst Rd EX2 11 H2
Marlborough Ct, Matford Business Pk EX2 16 D1
Marlborough Dr EX2 13 E2

Marlborough Rd EX2 11 H2
Marsh Barton Rd EX2 11 E4
Marsh Green Rd EX2 11 F4
Marsh La EX3 19 F3
Martins La EX1 3 C4
Marwood Rd EX6 9 B3
Mary Arches St EX4 3 B4
Maryfield Av EX4 5 G4
Marypole Rd EX4 6 A4
Marypole Walk EX4 6 A4
Masefield Rd EX4 6 D4
Matford Av EX2 11 H2
Matford La EX2 11 G3
Matford Park Rd EX2 11 G6
Matford Rd EX2 11 H2
Matthews St EX4 7 E3
May St EX4 5 H5
Mayfield Cl, Pinhoe EX4 7 F4
Mayfield Rd, St Loyes EX2 12 B2
Mayflower Av EX4 5 G2
Meadow Cl EX5 14 C4
Meadow Way EX2 12 A2
Meadowbrook Cl EX4 4 B5
Melbourne Pl EX2 3 D6
Melbourne St EX2 3 D6
Membury Cl EX1 13 E1
Mercer Ct EX2 12 B5
Merlin Cres EX4 6 B3
Mermaid Yard EX1 3 C5
Merrivale Rd EX4 10 C3
Michigan Way EX4 5 G2
Midway Ter EX2 11 E6
Milbury Cl EX6 17 H4
Milbury La EX6 17 H5
Mildmay Cl EX4 4 D6
Mile Gdns EX4 6 B3
Mile La EX4 6 B4
Milestones Cotts EX6 17 H6
Mill La, Clyst Honiton EX5 8 B4
Mill La, Countess Wear EX2 12 B6
Mill La, Exeter EX2 11 E6
Mill La, Exton EX3 20 B1
Mill Rd EX2 12 B6
Mill Yard EX2 12 A6
Millbrook La EX2 12 A5
Miller Cl EX2 12 D3
Miller Way EX6 17 G4
Milletts Cl EX4 17 H5
Millson Rd EX2 11 G3
Milton Rd EX2 12 A4
Minchinglake Rd EX4 6 A4
Minster Rd EX6 17 H4
Mission Ct EX4 3 B5
Mitre La EX4 3 B4
Modred Cl EX4 6 B4
Monitor Cl EX2 11 F3
Monkerton Dr EX1 7 F4
Monks Rd EX4 6 A5
Monkswell Rd EX4 5 H5
Monmouth Av EX3 19 E4
Monmouth Hill EX3 18 D5
Monmouth St EX3 19 E5
Mont Le Grand EX1 12 A1
Mont Le Grand Rd EX1 12 A1
Monterey Gdns EX4 5 H4
Montpelier Ct EX4 3 B2
Moon Ridge EX2 18 B2
Moonhill Cl EX2 16 D1
Moor La EX2 13 F1
Moorland Way EX4 4 C5
Moorview Cl EX4 5 H4
Morley Rd EX4 6 A5
Mortimer Ct EX2 12 B5
Mosshayne La EX1 7 H2
Mount Howe EX3 19 E5
Mount Pleasant Rd EX4 5 H5
Mount Radford Cres EX2 11 G2
Mount Wear Sq EX2 18 A1
Mowbray Av EX4 3 D2
Mulberry Cl EX1 6 D6
Musgrave Row EX4 3 C3
Mutton La EX4 6 D1
Myrtle Cl EX2 11 E6
Myrtle Rd EX4 10 C3

Nadder Park Rd EX4 10 B2
Napier Ter EX4 3 B4
Nelson Cl EX3 18 D4
Nelson Rd EX4 3 A6
Nelson Way EX2 13 E1
Neptune Ct EX1 3 C5
New Bridge St EX4 3 B5
New Buildings EX4 3 C3
New North Rd EX4 3 A1
New Valley Rd EX4 4 D6
Newcombe Gdns EX1 12 B1
Newcombe St EX1 12 B1
Newcourt Rd EX2 18 C1
Newfoundland Cl EX4 5 H2
Newhayes Cl EX2 10 D4
Newlands Cl EX4 10 D4
Newman Ct EX4 10 C2

Newman Rd EX4 10 C2
Newport Rd EX2 18 A2
Newtown Cl EX1 5 H6
Nicholas Rd EX1 12 B1
Nightingale Walk EX2 10 B4
Normandy Rd EX1 12 A1
North Av EX1 6 A6
North Bridge Pl EX4 3 B3
North Gate Ct EX4 3 B4
North Lawn Ct EX1 12 A1
North Park Rd EX4 5 F4
North St, Exeter EX4 3 C4
North St, Heavitree EX1 12 A1
North St, Topsham EX3 19 E5
Northernhay Gate EX4 3 C3
Northernhay Pl EX4 3 D3
Northernhay Sq EX4 3 B3
Northernhay St EX4 3 B4
Norwich Rd EX4 4 C6
Norwood Av EX2 11 G3
Nurseries Cl, Exton EX3 20 B1
Nurseries Cl, Topsham EX3 18 D3
Nutwell Rd EX8 20 D3

Oak Cl, Exminster EX6 17 H5
Oak Cl, Pinhoe EX1 7 F3
Oak Cl, Shillingford Abbot EX2 16 B3
Oak Rd EX4 10 C3
Oak Ridge EX2 16 B1
Oakfield Rd EX4 3 A6
Oakfield St EX1 12 A1
Oakley Cl EX1 7 F4
Oaktree Pl EX2 16 D1
Oberon Rd EX1 7 F6
Oil Mill La EX5 14 B5
Okehampton Pl EX4 3 A6
Okehampton Rd EX4 3 A5
Okehampton St EX4 3 A5
Old Abbey Ct EX2 11 H4
Old Bakery Cl EX4 4 D6
Old Dawlish Rd EX6 16 C6
Old Ebford La EX3 19 G5
Old Ide La EX2 10 C5
Old Market Cl EX2 11 F4
Old Matford La EX2 17 E3
Old Mill Cl EX2 11 G3
Old Park Rd EX4 3 D2
Old Pavilion Cl EX2 12 D3
Old Pinn La EX1 7 F4
Old Rydon Cl EX2 13 F5
Old Rydon La EX2 12 D6
Old Rydon Manor EX2 13 E5
Old Tiverton Rd EX4 5 G6
Old Vicarage Cl EX2 10 B6
Old Vicarage Rd EX2 10 D3
Olds Vw EX4 4 D5
Orchard Cl EX1 7 G3
Orchard Ct EX2 13 F1
Orchard Gdns EX4 10 C3
Orchard Hill EX4 10 C4
Orchard Way EX3 18 D3
Oriole Dr EX4 5 G3
Orwell Garth EX4 6 D4
Osprey Rd EX2 13 G1
Otter Ct EX2 16 D1
Oval Grn EX2 12 D3
Oxford Rd EX4 5 G6
Oxford St EX2 3 A6

Painters Ct EX2 3 C6
Palace Gate EX1 3 C5
Palmerston Dr EX4 4 C5
Pamela Rd EX1 6 A5
Paris St EX1 3 D3
Paris St Arcade EX1 3 D3
Park La EX4 7 E2
Park Pl, Heavitree EX1 12 A1
Park Pl, St Leonards EX2 11 G2
Park Rd EX1 6 A6
Parkers Cross La EX1 7 G3
Parkfield Rd EX3 18 D4
Parkhouse Rd EX2 10 D3
Parkland Dr EX2 12 D3
Parkside Cres EX1 7 G1
Parkside Rd EX1 7 G1
Parkway EX2 10 C4
Parliament St EX4 3 C4
Parr Cl EX1 5 H6
Parr St EX1 5 G6
Patricia Cl EX4 5 G3
Paul St EX4 3 C4
Pavilion Pl EX2 3 D5
Paynes Ct EX4 6 C5
Peel Cl EX3 18 D4
Peep La EX4 3 A3
Pellinore Rd EX4 6 B3
Pendragon Rd EX4 6 B3
Peninsula Pk EX2 12 D3
Penleonard Cl EX2 11 H2
Pennsylvania Cl EX4 5 G4
Pennsylvania Cres EX4 3 D1
Pennsylvania Pk EX4 5 G3
Pennsylvania Rd EX4 3 D2

Penny Cl EX6 17 H5
Penrose Ter EX1 3 C5
Perceval Rd EX4 6 B3
Percy Rd EX2 11 E4
Perridge Cl EX2 10 B4
Perry Rd EX4 3 B1
Peryam Cres EX2 12 B3
Peterborough Rd EX4 4 B6
Philip Rd EX4 6 A4
Piazza Terracina EX2 3 C6
Pilton La EX1 7 E4
Pinbrook Rd EX4 7 E4
Pinces Gdns EX2 11 E4
Pinces Rd EX2 11 E4
Pine Av EX4 4 C6
Pineridge Cl EX4 10 C3
Pinhoe Rd EX4 6 A5
Pinn Court La EX1 7 G3
Pinn Hill EX1 7 G3
Pinn La EX1 7 F4
Pinn Valley Rd EX1 7 G3
Pinwood La EX4 6 C3
Pinwood Meadow Dr EX4 6 C3
Pippin Cl EX1 6 D6
Plassey Cl EX4 5 G2
Playmoor Dr EX1 7 F3
Plumtree Dr EX2 12 C2
Pocombe Hill EX2 10 B4
Polehouse La EX2 10 C6
Polsloe Rd EX1 5 H5
Poltimore Rd EX1 7 H1
Poltimore Sq EX4 3 D3
Poplar Cl EX2 11 E4
Poppy Cl EX4 4 B5
Porters La EX8 20 C3
Portland Ho EX4 3 D3
Portland St EX1 5 H6
Post Office St EX1 3 D4
Pottles Ct EX6 17 H6
Pound Cl EX3 18 D3
Pound La EX3 18 D3
Powderham Cl EX3 18 C3
Powderham Cres EX4 3 D1
Powderham Rd EX2 10 D3
Premier Pl EX2 11 H2
Prescot Rd EX4 10 C2
Preston St EX1 3 C5
Pretoria Rd EX1 6 A6
Pridhams Way EX6 17 H4
Priestley Av EX4 6 C4
Primrose Lawn EX4 4 B5
Prince Charles Rd EX4 5 H4
Prince Of Wales Rd EX4 3 B1
Princes Sq EX2 11 E3
Princes St East EX2 11 E3
Princes St North EX2 11 E3
Princes St South EX2 11 E4
Princes St West EX2 11 E3
Princesshay EX1 3 D4
Priory Rd EX4 5 H5
Prison La EX4 3 C2
Prospect Gdns EX4 5 H5
Prospect Pk EX4 5 G5
Prospect Pl EX4 3 A6
Prospect Steps EX2 3 C5
Puckridge Rd EX4 7 E3
Puffin Way EX2 10 B3
Pulling Rd EX4 7 E3
Pulpit Walk EX2 16 D1
Purcell Cl EX2 12 D2
Pynes Hill EX2 12 D5
Pytte Gdns EX3 19 H2

Quarry La EX2 12 C2
Quarry Park Rd EX2 12 D3
Quay Hill EX1 3 C5
Quay La EX2 3 C5
Queen St EX4 3 B3
Queens Cres EX4 3 D2
Queens Rd EX2 11 E4
Queens Ter EX4 3 B2
Queensland Dr EX4 5 H2
Quintet Cl EX1 12 D1

Rack St EX1 3 C5
Rackfield Cotts EX4 4 C5
Radford Rd EX2 3 D6
Radnor Pl EX2 11 G2
Raglans EX2 16 D1
Raleigh Rd EX1 11 H1
Raven Cl EX4 5 G3
Rectory Dr EX2 11 F6
Red Cow Village EX4 3 A1
Red Lion La EX1 5 G6
Reddaway Dr EX6 17 G4
Redhills EX4 4 A6
Redhills Cl EX4 10 C1
Redlands Cl EX4 6 B5
Redvers Rd EX4 3 A5
Regent Sq EX1 12 B1
Regent St EX2 11 E4
Regents Pk EX1 12 A1
Rennes Dr EX4 5 F4
Renslade Ho EX4 3 B5

Retail Park Cl EX2
Retreat Rd EX3
Rews Mdw EX1
Rews Park Dr EX1
Rexona Cl EX4
Reynolds Cl EX4
Ribston Av EX1
Rices Mews EX2
Richmond Rd EX4
Ridgeway EX4
Rifford Rd EX2
Ringswell Av EX1
Ripon Cl EX4
River Front EX3
River Mdws EX2
Rivermead Rd EX2
Rivers Walk EX2
Riverside Ct EX2
Riverside Rd EX3
Riversmeet EX3
Riverview Dr EX4
Riverview Ter EX6
Riviera Ter EX6
Roberts Rd EX2
Roche Gdn EX2
Rockside EX4
Rockside Villas EX4
Rollestone Cres EX4
Roly-Poly Hill EX2
Romsey Dr EX2
Rosebank Cres EX4
Rosebarn Av EX4
Rosebarn La EX4
Rosebery Rd EX4
Roseland Av EX1
Roseland Dr EX1
Rosemary St EX4
Rosemont Ct EX2
Rosewood Cres EX5
Rosewood Ter EX4
Ross Cl EX1
Rougemont Ct EX6
Round Table Meet EX4
Roundhill Cl EX4
Rowan Way EX4
Rowhorne Rd EX4
Royal Cl EX2
Royston Ct EX1
Rugby Rd EX4
Rushforth Pl EX4
Russell St EX1
Russell Ter EX4
Russell Way EX2
Russet Av EX1
Russet Cl EX1
Rutherford St EX2
Rydon La, Exeter EX2
Rydon La, Exton EX3
Rydon Pk EX2

St Albans Cl EX4
St Andrews Rd EX4
St Annes Rd EX1
St Annes Well Mews EX4
St Bernards Cl EX2
St Clements La EX4
St Davids Hill EX4
St Davids Ter EX4
St Germans Rd EX4
St Hill Cl EX2
St Idas Cl EX2
St James Cl EX4
St James Ct EX1
St James Rd EX4
St James Ter EX4
St Johns Rd EX4
St Katherines Rd EX4
St Leonards Av EX2
St Leonards Pl, Clyst St Mary EX5
St Leonards Pl, Exeter EX2
St Leonards Rd EX2
St Loyes Rd EX2
St Loyes Ter EX2
St Margarets Ter EX3
St Marks Av EX1
St Mary Step Ter EX1
St Mathews Cl EX1
St Michaels Cl, Clyst Honiton EX5
St Michaels Cl, Exeter EX2
St Michaels Hill EX5
St Peters Mount EX4
St Petrocks Cl EX2
St Sidwells Av EX4
St Thomas Ct EX4
Salem Pl EX1
Salisbury Rd EX4
Salmon Pool La EX2
Salters Ct EX2
Salters Rd EX2
Salutary Mount EX1
Sampsons La EX1
Sanders Rd EX4

ord Walk EX1 5 H6
piper Ct EX4 7 E3
piper Dr EX3 20 B1
piper Grn EX2 10 B3
ygate EX2 13 G4
erville Way EX6 17 H3
ent Cl EX1 12 D1
e Rd EX4 10 D2
y Hill EX4 6 B3
n Av EX4 7 F3
n Rd EX1 12 B1
ol La EX2 12 B6
ol Rd EX2 11 E3
Av EX2 12 A4
ch Face La EX2 10 A5
ook Av EX2 18 A2
nd Av, Exeter EX1 12 A1
nd Av,
wport Pk EX2 18 B2
eclaire EX1 7 G3
ys Orch EX6 18 A6
e Ct EX2 3 C6
esbury Rd EX2 10 D3
espeare Rd EX2 12 A4
man Ct EX2 3 C6
ey Cl EX2 10 D4
pard Rd EX4 5 G3
roft Cl EX5 8 D3
dan Rd EX4 6 D4
vood Cl EX2 12 A2
ngford La EX6 16 B5
ngford Rd EX2 16 C2
La EX5 8 C5
king Marsh Stile
2 3 B6
outh Rd,
rst St Mary EX5 14 B5
outh Rd,
ster EX2 13 E2
ell St EX4 3 D3
e Birch Cl EX2 12 B3
r La EX4 5 H6
r Ter EX4 3 B3
rton Rd EX2 17 E1
ex Walk EX3 18 C3
Mews EX2 12 B2
Pl EX2 12 A2
y Hollow EX2 18 B2
n Field Rd EX2 16 B1
afield Rd EX2 11 E6
hen St EX1 3 C5
drop Mews EX4 4 B5
Cres EX4 10 C3
erset Av EX4 10 B3
a Av EX1 6 A6
a Lawn Ter EX1 12 A1
a St EX1 3 C4
a View Ter,
ster EX4 5 G5
a View Ter,
minster EX6 17 H5
abrook Rd EX2 12 B5
ernhay East EX1 3 D5
ernhay Gdns
1 3 D5
ernhay West EX1 3 D5
sgate EX2 3 C5
sport Av EX2 10 C2
on La EX5 7 H6
on La EX5 8 A6
ser Av EX2 12 A4
r Rd EX1 11 G1
ey Cl EX2 12 D3
ring Fld EX4 5 H5
gfield Rd EX4 5 G5
te Cl EX4 6 C2
vay Hill EX6 17 G6
on Cl EX4 6 C6
rd Rd EX4 10 D2
ord Rd EX2 12 D2
ey Sq EX3 18 D4
vey EX1 12 B1
Barton La EX4 4 A1
n Rd,
adclyst EX5 8 C1
n Rd, Exeter EX4 3 A1
n Rd,
minster EX6 18 A6
n Rd, Exton EX3 20 B2
n Rd, Ide EX2 10 B6
n Rd, Pinhoe EX1 7 F3
n Rd,
osham EX3 18 D4
n Yd EX4 3 B3
le Dr EX2 16 C1
ote Hill EX1 3 B5
Cl EX1 7 F4
g Ho EX1 3 D4
er Rd EX4 5 E4
Hill EX4 5 H4
Hill Cres EX4 5 H4
Meadow Cl EX4 5 H3
Rd EX4 4 D1
Valley Rd EX4 5 G2
La EX8 20 E3

Stover Ct EX1 5 G6
Strand Ct EX4 18 D5
Strand Vw EX3 19 E5
Stratford Av EX4 7 E4
Strawberry Av EX2 16 D1
Stream Ct EX2 3 C6
Streatham Dr EX4 3 B1
Streatham Rise EX4 3 B1
Stuart Rd EX1 12 B1
Sullivan Rd EX2 12 D2
Summer Cl EX4 6 C5
Summer La EX4 6 C3
Summerland St EX1 5 G6
Summerway EX4 6 C5
Sunhill Av EX3 18 D3
Sunhill La EX3 18 D3
Sunnymoor Cl EX1 7 G3
Surbiton Cres EX4 10 C3
Sussex Cl EX4 10 B3
Swains Ct EX3 18 D4
Swallow Ct EX4 4 D4
Swallow Dr EX2 10 B3
Swallowfield Rd EX2 12 C5
Swan Ct EX2 11 G3
Swan Yd EX4 3 B6
Sweetbrier La EX1 6 B6
Sycamore Cl EX1 12 C2
Sydney Rd EX2 11 E3
Sylvan Av EX4 5 H4
Sylvan Rd EX4 5 H4
Sylvania Dr EX4 5 H2
Taddiforde Rd EX4 3 A1
Taddyforde Ct EX4 3 A1
Taddyforde Est EX4 3 A1
Tamarisk Cl EX4 6 C2
Tan La EX2 11 F3
Tappers Cl EX4 18 D3
Taps Cl EX6 17 H5
Tarbet Av EX1 6 B5
Taunton Cl EX2 11 E4
Tavistock Rd EX4 3 A2
Teazle Ct EX4 3 C6
Teazle Ct EX2 11 F2
Tedburn Rd EX4 10 A2
Tedstone Rd EX8 20 F4
Telford Rd EX4 3 A2
Temple Rd EX2 3 D5
Tennyson Av EX2 12 A4
Thackeray Rd EX4 6 D5
The College EX2 10 B5
The Copse EX2 18 B2
The Fairway EX4 5 H3
The Green EX2 10 B5
The Hams EX2 10 B5
The Maltings EX2 12 A1
The Mede, Exeter EX4 6 D5
The Mede,
Topsham EX3 18 D4
The Mint EX4 3 B4
The Panney EX4 6 B5
The Poplars EX4 7 F3
The Quarries EX4 10 B3
The Quay EX2 3 C6
The Queens Dr EX4 5 E4
The Retreat Dr EX3 18 C2
The Ridings EX3 19 G4
The Shrubbery EX3 18 D4
The Square EX4 4 D5
The Strand EX3 18 D5
The Triangles EX1 11 G1
The Village EX5 13 H4
The Wicket EX2 12 D3
Third Av, Exeter EX1 6 A6
Third Av,
Newport Pk EX2 18 B2
Third Av,
Ringswell Pk EX2 13 E1
Thomas La EX4 3 A1
Thompson Rd EX1 6 B5
Thorn Cl EX1 12 C1
Thornberry Av EX1 12 C1
Thorndale Cts EX4 4 B4
Thornpark Rise EX1 6 C6
Thornton Hill EX4 3 D1
Three Corner Pl EX2 16 D1
Thurlow Rd EX4 5 H5
Tin La EX2 10 D3
Tintagel Cl EX4 6 B3
Tithebarn Copse EX1 7 G4
Tithebarn La EX1 7 F5
Tollards Rd EX2 12 B5
Topsham Rd EX2 3 D6
Tor Cl EX4 6 B4
Toronto Rd EX4 5 H5
Tottons Ct EX2 16 C1
Tower Walk EX2 16 D1
Towerfield EX3 18 D2
Townfield EX2 16 C1
Towsington La EX6 17 G6
Trafalgar Pl EX4 5 G5
Trafford Mews EX4 12 D3
Trentbridge Sq EX2 12 D3
Tresillian Cotts EX3 19 E6
Tresillian Gdns,

Tresillian Gdns,
Topsham EX3 19 E5
Trews Weir Reach EX2 11 G3
Trinity Ct EX1 3 D4
Tristan Ct EX4 6 B3
Trood La EX2 17 E3
Truro Dr EX4 4 C6
Trusham Rd EX2 11 F4
Tuckfield Cl EX2 12 B3
Tudor Ct EX4 3 B5
Tudor St EX4 3 B5
Tuffery Ct EX4 6 A5
Tugela Ter EX5 13 H4
Two Acre Ct EX2 16 B1
Underhill Ter EX3 18 D4
Union Rd EX4 5 G5
Union St EX2 3 A6
Uplands Dr EX4 6 B4
Upper Paul St EX4 3 C3
Vachell Cres EX2 13 E1
Valley Park Cl EX4 5 G2
Valley Rd,
Cat & Fiddle Pk EX5 14 C4
Valley Rd, Exeter EX4 4 D5
Varco Sq EX2 12 D3
Vaughan Rd EX1 6 C6
Vaughan Rise EX1 6 C6
Veitch Gdns EX2 16 C1
Velwell Rd EX4 3 B2
Venny Bridge EX4 7 E4
Verney St EX1 5 G6
Vestry Dr EX2 16 C1
Vicarage Gdns EX2 10 D3
Vicarage La EX4 7 F2
Victor Cl EX1 12 B1
Victor La EX1 12 B1
Victor St EX1 12 B1
Victoria Park Rd EX2 11 H2
Victoria Rd, Exeter EX4 5 G5
Victoria Rd,
Topsham EX3 18 D4
Victoria St EX4 5 G5
Victoria Yard EX4 3 C3
Vine Cl EX2 11 G2
Vuefield Hill EX2 10 C4
Waggoners Way EX4 4 D5
Wallace Av EX4 6 D5
Walnut Cl EX6 17 H5
Walnut Gdns EX4 3 A2
Walnut Rd EX2 12 B4
Walpole Cl EX4 6 D4
Walton Rd EX2 12 B4
Wardrew Rd EX4 10 D2
Warren La EX4 3 D2
Warwick Av EX1 12 D1
Warwick Rd EX1 12 D1
Warwick Way EX4 6 D4
Water La EX2 3 C6
Waterbeer St EX4 3 C4
Watergate EX2 3 C5
Waterloo Rd EX2 11 E4
Waterside EX2 3 C6
Waterslade La EX5 8 C5
Waverley Av EX4 3 C2
Waybrook Cres EX2 11 F6
Waybrook La EX2 16 B3
Wayland Av EX2 11 G2
Wayside Cres EX1 6 C6
Wear Barton Rd EX2 18 A1
Wear Cl EX2 18 A2
Weavers Ct EX2 3 C6
Webley Rd EX2 10 D4
Weirfield Rd EX2 3 D6
Welcome St EX2 11 F3
Well Oak Pk EX2 12 A3
Well St EX4 5 G6
Wellington Cl EX2 13 E1
Wellington Rd EX2 11 E4
Wellpark Cl EX2 10 C1
Wellswood Gdns EX4 10 C1
Wendover Way EX2 12 C5
Wentworth Gdns EX4 3 D1
Wesley Cl EX2 11 E4
Wesley Way EX2 16 C1
Wessex Cl EX3 18 C3
West Av EX4 3 D1
West Clyst EX1 7 G2
West Garth Rd EX4 6 B3
West Grove Rd EX2 11 G2
West St EX1 3 B5
West View Ter EX4 3 B4
Westbrook Cl EX4 5 H4
Westcombe EX2 16 C1
Western Rd EX4 3 A4
Western Way EX1 3 C5
Western Way EX1 11 F2
Western Way EX1 11 G1
Westfield EX6 18 A6
Westminster Rd EX4 4 B6
Westown Rd EX2 10 A6
Westwood La EX6 10 A3
Weycroft Cl EX1 12 E1
Wheatley Cl EX4 10 B2

Wheatley Ct EX1 3 C5
Wheatsheaf Way EX2 11 E6
Whiddon La EX2 10 A6
Whipton Barton Rd EX1 6 C5
Whipton La EX1 12 B6
Whipton Rd EX4 6 B5
Whipton Village Rd EX4 6 C5
Whitchurch Av EX2 12 C3
White St EX3 18 D5
Whitebeam Cl EX4 6 C3
Whitehall La EX3 18 D1
Whiteside Cl EX2 12 D3
Whitethorn Pk EX4 5 G2
Whiteway Dr EX1 12 C1
Whitlow Copse EX2 12 D3
Whitycombe Way EX4 4 B4
Widecombe Way EX4 5 H3
Widgery Rd EX4 6 B5
Wilcocks Rd EX4 7 E4
Wilford Rd EX2 12 C2
Willeys Av EX2 11 E3
Williams Av EX2 3 B6
Willow Ct EX2 12 B3
Willow Walk EX4 5 G5
Willsdown Rd EX2 16 D1
Wiltshire Cl EX4 10 C3
Wilton Way EX1 13 E1
Winchester Av EX4 4 C6
Windermere Cl EX4 10 D1
Windsor Cl EX4 3 A2
Winkleigh Cl EX2 11 E4
Winslade Park Av EX5 13 H5
Wonford Rd EX2 11 G2
Wonford St EX2 12 B2
Woodah Rd EX4 10 D2
Woodbine Ter EX4 3 B2
Woodbury Rd EX8 20 D3
Woodbury Vw EX2 10 D5
Woodland Rd EX1 7 E6
Woodlands Way EX5 14 C4
Woodleigh Cl EX4 5 E2
Woodstock Rd EX2 12 C2
Woodville Rd EX2 11 F4
Woodwater La EX2 12 C2
Woodwater La EX2 12 C3
Woodwater La EX2 12 D4
Woolaway Av EX6 18 A5
Woolsery Av EX4 6 C4
Woolsery Ct EX4 6 C4
Woolsery Gro EX4 6 C4
Wrefords Cl EX4 4 D2
Wrefords Dr EX4 4 D2
Wrefords La EX4 4 D1
Wykes Rd EX1 6 A5
Wynards La EX2 3 D5
Wyndham Av EX1 12 B3
Wynford Rd EX4 6 A4
Yeoford Way EX2 17 E1
Yew Tree Cl EX4 5 H4
York Rd EX4 3 D2
York Ter EX4 5 G6

EXMOUTH

Admirals Walk EX8 23 E1
Albany Cl EX8 23 F1
Albert Pl EX8 22 C4
Albion Hill EX8 22 C4
Albion Pl EX8 22 C4
Albion St EX8 22 C4
Aldborough Ct EX8 22 D5
Alexandra Ter EX8 22 B5
Alston Ter EX8 22 A5
Ann St EX8 22 C4
Anson Rd EX8 24 B4
Apple Cl EX8 24 A3
April Cl EX8 24 A4
Ardenney Ct EX8 22 D5
Arthurs Cl EX8 22 C4
Ash Gro EX8 24 A4
Ashfield Cl EX8 23 G1
Ashleigh Rd EX8 22 C3
Avondale Rd EX8 23 E2
Bakery La EX8 22 C3
Bankside EX8 24 B3
Bapton Cl EX8 22 D1
Bapton La EX8 22 C1
Barnfield Av EX8 23 E3
Barrowdale Cl EX8 24 C3
Bassetts Gdns EX8 23 F1
Bath Rd EX8 22 B5
Beacon Pl EX8 22 B5
Beechway EX8 22 C2
Belle Vue Rd EX8 22 B2
Belvedere Rd EX8 22 C3
Berry Cl EX8 23 F3
Bicton Cl EX8 22 B5
Bicton St EX8 22 B4
Bicton Villas EX8 22 C4
Bidmead Cl EX8 23 F3
Birch Rd EX8 21 D6
Birchwood Rd EX8 24 C4

Blackmore Ct EX8 23 F2
Blue Cedar Ct EX8 22 D4
Boarden Barn EX8 22 C4
Booth Way EX8 24 A4
Brackendale EX8 24 B3
Brackenwood EX8 23 E2
Bradford Cl EX8 24 B3
Bradham Ct EX8 23 E2
Bradham La EX8 23 E2
Breton Way EX8 23 F2
Briar Cl EX8 23 F3
Bridge Rd EX8 22 C3
Brimpenny Rd EX8 23 E1
Brittany Rd EX8 24 B3
Brixington Dr EX8 23 E1
Brixington La EX8 24 C4
Broadmead EX8 24 C4
Broadpark Rd EX8 23 E1
Brookhayes Cl EX8 22 D2
Brooklands Rd EX8 23 E2
Buckingham Cl EX8 23 F3
Bunn Rd EX8 24 C3
Burch Cl EX8 23 F1
Burgmanns Hill EX8 21 C5
Burnside EX8 22 D2
Byron Way EX8 24 B3
Bystock Mews EX8 24 D3
Bystock Rd EX8 24 D3
Camperdown Ter EX8 22 A4
Canterbury Way EX8 24 D3
Capel La EX8 23 G2
Carberry Av EX8 22 B1
Carlton Hill EX8 22 C5
Caroline Ct EX8 23 E2
Carter Av EX8 22 B2
Castle La EX8 23 H3
Caulston Cl EX8 22 C1
Cedar Cl EX8 24 C3
Chapel Hill EX8 22 B4
Chapel St EX8 22 B4
Chaplel La EX8 21 C6
Charles St EX8 22 C4
Chatham Cl EX8 23 F2
Cheriswood Av EX8 23 E1
Cherry Cl EX8 24 B3
Cheshire Rd EX8 23 F1
Chestnut Cl EX8 24 B4
Chichester Cl EX8 22 D3
Chudley Cl EX8 23 E2
Church Rd,
Exmouth EX8 22 B3
Church Rd,
Lympstone EX8 21 D6
Churchill Ct EX8 21 D5
Churchill Rd EX8 24 C4
Claredale Rd EX8 22 D4
Claremont Gro EX8 22 D4
Claremont La EX8 22 D4
Clarence Rd EX8 22 C4
Clay La EX8 21 D6
Clerk Cl EX8 23 E1
Cleveland Pl EX8 22 B4
Clinton Sq EX8 22 B5
Cliston Av EX8 24 D4
Coleridge Cl EX8 24 B3
Colleton Cl EX8 23 E3
Colleton Way EX8 23 E3
Colvin Cl EX8 23 F4
Combourg Ct EX8 23 E4
Comilla Cl EX8 24 B3
Concorde Rd EX8 23 G2
Copperfield Cl EX8 23 F2
Courtlands La EX8 21 E7
Cranford Av EX8 22 D5
Cranford Cl EX8 22 D4
Cranford Vw EX8 22 D4
Crossingfields Dr EX8 22 D3
Crowders Hill EX8 24 A3
Cumberland Cl EX8 23 F2
Cunningham Rd EX8 23 E1
Cyprus Rd EX8 22 D4
Dagmar Rd EX8 22 C5
Danby La EX8 22 C3
Danby Ter EX8 22 C5
Dawlish Park Ter EX8 21 D7
Delderfield Gdns EX8 22 D4
Dene Ct EX8 22 B6
Denmark Rd EX8 23 E2
Denning Ct EX8 22 D2
Diane Cl EX8 24 C3
Dinan Way EX8 24 D4
Dorchester Way EX8 24 C2
Douglas Av EX8 22 C5
Douglas St EX8 23 E5
Drakes Av EX8 23 E3
Drakes Gdns EX8 23 F2
Duke of Cornwall Cl EX8 23 F1
Dukes Cres EX8 23 F2
Dunsford Cl EX8 23 E4
Durham Cl EX8 24 C3
East Dr EX8 22 C1
Edinburgh Cres EX8 21 D6

Egremont Rd EX8 22 B3
Elizabeth Rd EX8 22 D1
Ellwood Rd EX8 24 C4
Elm Gro EX8 22 B4
Elm La EX8 23 G3
Elm Rd EX8 22 D4
Elmdene Ct EX8 22 D4
Elmfield Cres EX8 21 F8
Elvis Rd EX8 23 E3
Elwyn Rd EX8 23 E4
Emmasfield EX8 23 E3
Esplanade EX8 22 A5
Essington Cl EX8 24 A4
Estuary Ct EX8 22 A4
Evergreen Cl EX8 24 C3
Evett Cl EX8 23 F2
Exe View Rd EX8 24 B1
Exeter Rd EX8 21 F7
Exmouth Ct EX8 22 D4
Exmouth Rd EX8 21 E5

Fairfield Cl EX8 22 C5
Fairfield Rd EX8 22 C5
Fairview Ter EX8 22 C3
Featherbed La EX8 21 F8
Featherstone Rd EX8 22 C1
Fir Tree Cl EX8 24 E4
Fore St EX8 22 B4
Forton Rd EX8 23 E2
Foxholes Hill EX8 23 E6
Fraser Rd EX8 23 E1
Freelands Cl EX8 23 E2
Frobisher Rd EX8 24 B4

Garratt Cl EX8 24 B3
George St EX8 22 C4
Gibraltar Rd EX8 21 D5
Gibson Cl EX8 23 F1
Gipsy La EX8 22 C2
Glebe Cl,
  Exmouth EX8 23 G3
Glebe Cl,
  Lympstone EX8 21 D5
Glebelands EX8 21 D5
Gloucester Rd EX8 24 D3
Gore La EX8 23 F5
Gorfin Cl EX8 23 F2
Gorse La EX8 24 C3
Grange Av EX8 22 C2
Grange Cl,
  Exmouth EX8 22 C2
Grange Cl,
  Lympstone EX8 21 E5
Green Cl EX8 22 D2
Greenhill Av,
  Exmouth EX8 22 D4
Greenhill Av,
  Lympstone EX8 21 D6
Greenpark Rd EX8 24 C4
Grenville Rd EX8 24 B4
Gussiford La EX8 22 C4

Hadrians Way EX8 23 F2
Haldon Ct EX8 22 C1
Haley Rd EX8 24 B4
Halsdon Av EX8 22 B2
Halsdon La EX8 22 B1
Halsdon Rd EX8 22 B3
Hamilton La EX8 22 D3
Hamilton Rd EX8 23 E3
Harbour Ct EX8 22 A4
Harefield EX8 21 E6
Hartley Rd EX8 22 C5
Hartopp Rd EX8 22 B3
Harwood Cl EX8 23 E1
Hawthorn Gro EX8 23 F1
Hazeldene Gdns EX8 22 C2
Heard Av EX8 23 F2
Heatherdale EX8 22 D4
Helena Pl EX8 22 C4
Henley Rd EX8 23 E3
Henrietta Rd EX8 22 C4
Hereford Cl EX8 24 C3
Heron Ct EX8 22 D5
High St EX8 22 B4
Highbury Pk EX8 22 B1
Highcliffe Cl EX8 21 C6
Highcliffe Ct EX8 21 C6
Higher Marley Rd EX8 24 C2
Highfield EX8 22 C5
Highview Gdns EX8 22 C2
Hill Dr EX8 24 A3
Holland Rd EX8 23 E2
Holly Mount Cl EX8 24 B3
Holly Walk EX8 24 C3
Hulham Rd EX8 22 C2
Humphries Pk EX8 23 F1
Hunton Cl EX8 21 D5

Imperial Rd EX8 22 B4

INDUSTRIAL & RETAIL:
Dinan Way Trading Est
  EX8 23 G2
Liverton Business Pk
  EX8 23 G1
Pound La Industrial Est
  EX8 22 D2

Iona Av EX8 22 C1
Isca Rd EX8 22 D5
Ivydale EX8 24 C4

Jarvis Cl EX8 23 F3
Jubilee Dr EX8 24 B4
Jubilee Gro EX8 21 E6

Kay Cl EX8 22 D2
Keats Cl EX8 24 B3
Keverel Rd EX8 22 C1
Kincraig EX8 23 E4
King St EX8 22 B4
Kingslake Ct EX8 22 B2
Kingston Rd EX8 23 E3

Laburnum Cl EX8 24 C3
Lamplough Rd EX8 21 F8
Langerwehe Way EX8 22 A4
Langstone Dr EX8 22 D1
Larch Cl EX8 24 C3
Laurel Rise EX8 23 E3
Lawn Rd EX8 22 C3
Leslie Rd EX8 22 C3
Lestock Cl EX8 23 G3
Lime Gro EX8 24 B4
Limekiln La EX8 22 D5
Lincoln Cl EX8 24 D3
Linden Cl EX8 23 E1
Links Cl EX8 22 D3
Little Bicton Pl EX8 22 B4
Little Mdw EX8 24 D4
Littledown Cl EX8 23 G3
Littleham Rd EX8 23 F3
Littlemead La EX8 21 F7
Liverton Cl EX8 23 G2
Long Causeway EX8 22 C4
Long La EX8 22 D4
Longbrook La EX8 21 E6
Longmeadow Rd EX8 21 D6
Louisa Pl EX8 22 C5
Louisa Ter EX8 22 B5
Lovelace Cres EX8 23 E2
Lovell Cl EX8 24 B4
Lyndhurst Rd EX8 22 C2

Madagascar Cl EX8 23 F2
Madeira Ct EX8 22 C5
Madeira Villas EX8 22 C3
Maer Bay Ct EX8 22 D5
Maer La EX8 22 D5
Maer Rd EX8 22 D5
Maer Vale EX8 22 D5
Magnolia Av EX8 23 F3
Malt Field EX8 21 E6
Mamhead Vw EX8 22 A5
Manchester Rd EX8 22 B4
Manchester St EX8 22 B4
Maple Dr EX8 24 C3
Marcom Cl EX8 24 C3
Marcus Rd EX8 23 E1
Marina Ct EX8 22 D5
Marine Way EX8 22 B4
Marions Way EX8 24 C4
Maristow Av EX8 22 C1
Market St EX8 22 B4
Marlborough Cl EX8 24 D4
Marley Dr EX8 24 C1
Marley Rd EX8 24 A4
Marley Rd EX8 24 C3
Marpool Cres EX8 22 D3
Marpool Hill EX8 23 E4
Martins Rd EX8 24 D4
Masey Rd EX8 23 E2
Mayfield Dr EX8 23 E5
Mead Cotts EX8 23 G4
Meadow Cl EX8 21 E6
Meadow St EX8 22 C4
Meadow View Rd EX8 23 F1
Meeting La EX8 21 D5
Meeting St EX8 22 C4
Meetways La EX8 23 E5
Meresyke EX8 23 E4
Merrion Av EX8 23 E4
Midway EX8 23 F3
Montpellier Ct EX8 22 C4
Montpellier Rd EX8 22 C4
Moorfield Cl EX8 22 D2

Moorfield Rd EX8 22 D2
Moorpark EX8 22 D5
Morton Cres EX8 22 A5
Morton Cres Mews EX8 22 B5
Morton Rd EX8 22 B4
Morven Dr EX8 22 C1
Mount Pleasant Av EX8 24 A4
Mountain Cl EX8 23 G2
Mountbatten Cl EX8 23 E1
Mudbank La EX8 22 B2
Myrtle Row EX8 22 C5

Nasmith Cl EX8 23 E1
Nelson Dr EX8 23 F3
New North Rd EX8 22 B4
New St EX8 22 B4
Newlands Av EX8 23 E2
Norman Cl EX8 23 E4
Norman Stevens Cl EX8 22 D4
Normandy Cl EX8 23 G1
North St EX8 22 C4
Norwich Cl EX8 24 C3
Nursery Cl EX8 22 D2
Nursery Mews EX8 22 D2
Nutbrook EX8 22 D1
Nutwell Rd EX8 21 D5

Oakleigh Rd EX8 22 D3
Oaktree Cl EX8 24 A3
Oakwood Rise EX8 24 D3
Okewood Ct EX8 22 D5
Old Bystock Dr EX8 24 D3
Oldfields EX8 22 D4
Orchard Cl,
  Exmouth EX8 22 C1
Orchard Cl,
  Lympstone EX8 21 D5
Orcombe Ct EX8 23 F3
Oxford Cl EX8 24 D3

Palm Cl EX8 24 C3
Pankhurst Cl EX8 23 G3
Parade EX8 22 B4
Park La EX8 22 C3
Park Rd EX8 22 C3
Park Way EX8 22 D3
Parkside Dr EX8 24 C4
Parson Cl EX8 23 E1
Parthia Pl EX8 23 F2
Partridge Rd EX8 24 B4
Pentegrove Ct EX8 23 E4
Phear Av EX8 22 D4
Phillipps Av EX8 22 C1
Pier Head EX8 22 A5
Pine View Cl EX8 24 E4
Pines Rd EX8 24 C3
Point Ter EX8 22 A4
Poplar Cl EX8 24 C3
Port Mer Cl EX8 24 D4
Portland Av EX8 22 C5
Pound La EX8 23 E1
Pound St EX8 22 C4
Priddis Cl EX8 24 B4
Prince Charles Cl EX8 23 F2
Prince of Wales Dr EX8 23 F2

Quay La EX8 21 C6
Queen St EX8 22 B4
Queens Dr EX8 22 C6

Raddenstile Ct EX8 22 D4
Raddenstile La EX8 22 C4
Raleigh Rd EX8 22 C4
Randalls Grn EX8 23 F4
Read Cl EX8 22 D1
Redwood Cl EX8 24 C3
Regency Cres EX8 24 D4
Regents Gate EX8 22 C4
Rhyll Cl EX8 22 D4
Richards Cl EX8 24 C4
Richmond Rd EX8 23 E3
Rivermead Av EX8 21 F8
Rodney Cl EX8 23 H4
Rolle Rd EX8 22 C4
Rolle St EX8 22 B4
Rolle Villas EX8 22 C5
Rosebery Rd EX8 22 B3
Roseway EX8 23 G2
Roundhouse La EX8 24 A4
Rowlstone Cl EX8 24 B3
Ryll Court Dr EX8 22 C3
Ryll Gro EX8 22 C3

Sadler Cl EX8 23 F2
St Andrews Rd EX8 22 A5
St Johns Ct EX8 23 E1
St Johns Farm Mews
  EX8 24 E3

St Johns Rd EX8 23 E2
St Johns Rd EX8 24 E4
St Malo Cl EX8 24 D3
St Margarets Vw EX8 23 H3
St Sevan Way EX8 24 D4
Salisbury Rd EX8 22 B3
Salterton Rd EX8 22 C5
Sarlsdown Rd EX8 23 E4
Scarsdale EX8 23 E5
School Hill EX8 21 D5
School La EX8 22 D2
Schooners Ct EX8 22 A4
Scott Dr EX8 24 A4
Seafield Av EX8 21 F8
Senate Way EX8 23 F2
Seymour Ct EX8 22 C1
Seymour Rd EX8 22 C1
Shackleton Cl EX8 24 A4
Shakespeare Way EX8 24 B3
Sharps Ct EX8 22 A4
Shelley Ct EX8 22 A5
Shelley Rd EX8 22 A4
Shelly Rd EX8 22 A4
Shelly Reach EX8 22 A4
Sheppards Row EX8 22 B4
Sherwood Dr EX8 24 D4
Shirley Cl EX8 24 C2
Silverdale EX8 24 D4
Somerville Cl EX8 23 E1
South St EX8 22 B4
Southern Rd EX8 22 B2
Southern Wood Cl EX8 24 E4
Sovereign Cl EX8 23 F2
Sowden La EX8 21 C6
Spencer Cl EX8 24 D4
Springfield Rd EX8 22 C2
Spruce Cl EX8 24 C3
Spyders La EX8 24 B4
Stanley Walk EX8 24 D3
Stevenstone Rd EX8 23 E3
Stewart Cl EX8 23 F2
Stone La EX8 21 D6
Strand EX8 22 B4
Strawberry Hill EX8 21 D6
Sturges Rd EX8 23 F2
Summer Cl EX8 23 F3
Summer La EX8 21 F7
Sunwine Pl EX8 22 C5
Swiss Cl EX8 24 A3
Sycamore Cl EX8 23 F1
Sylvan Cl EX8 21 F8

Tedstone La EX8 21 F5
Tennyson Way EX8 24 B3
The Beacon EX8 22 B5
The Broadway EX8 23 F3
The Copse EX8 24 D4
The Crescent EX8 23 F3
The Green EX8 23 G3
The Hollows EX8 22 C3
The Marles EX8 22 D1
The Royal Av EX8 22 B4
The Strand,
  Exmouth EX8 22 B4
The Strand,
  Lympstone EX8 21 C6
Thomas Cl, Exeter EX8 24 B3
Thomas Cl,
  Foxholes Hill EX8 23 F6
Thornfield Cl EX8 21 F8
Thorpe Av EX8 24 A3
Tower St EX8 22 B4
Trafalgar Rd EX8 21 D5
Travershes Cl EX8 22 D1
Trefusis Pl EX8 22 C5
Trefusis Ter EX8 22 C5
Trinfield Av EX8 22 C1
Truro Dr EX8 24 C3
Turner Av EX8 22 D4

Underhill Cl EX8 21 C6
Underhill Cl EX8 21 D6
Underhill Cres EX8 21 D6
Union St EX8 22 C4
Upper Church St EX8 22 C4

Vale EX8 23 E3
Valley Way EX8 24 D3
Vansittart Dr EX8 24 B4
Vernon Rd EX8 23 E4
Victoria Pl EX8 22 C4
Victoria Rd EX8 22 A5
Victoria Way EX8 22 A4
Village Cl EX8 23 G3

Wade Cl EX8 23 F2
Walls Cl EX8 24 C4
Walnut Gro EX8 23 E4

Warneford Gdns EX8
Waverley Rd EX8
Wells Cl EX8
West Down La EX8
Westlands EX8
Westminster Cl EX8
Westward Dr EX8
White Stones EX8
Whitman Cl EX8
Willoughby Cl EX8
Willow Av EX8
Wilmot Cl EX8
Winchester Dr EX8
Windsor Sq EX8
Winston Rd EX8
Withycombe Park Dr
  EX8
Withycombe Village Rd
  EX8
Woodbury Ct EX8
Woodfield Cl EX8
Woodlands Dr EX8
Woodville Rd EX8
Wordsworth Cl EX8
Wotton La EX8
Wrights La EX8

Yew Tree Cl EX8
York Cl EX8

WOODBURY

Beeches Cl EX5
Bonds La EX5
Bonfire La EX5
Brent Cl EX5
Brettevile Cl EX5
Broadmead EX5
Broadway EX5

Castle La EX5
Church Stile La EX5
Cottles La EX5
Couches La EX5
Critchards EX5
Culvery Cl EX5
Culvery La EX5

Flower St EX5
Fulford Way EX5
Furze Rd EX5

Gilbrook EX5
Globe Hill EX5
Govetts EX5
Greenway EX5

Hayes Orch EX5

Long Mdw EX5
Long Pk EX5

Mirey La EX5

Oakhayes Rd EX5
Orchard Cl EX5

Park Cl EX5
Park Way EX5
Parsonage Way EX5
Pound La EX5

Rydon EX5
Rydon La EX5

Stokes Mead EX5
Summerfield EX5

The Arch EX5
Town La EX5

Watery La EX5
White Cross Rd EX5
Woodbury Rd EX5
Woodbury Rd EX5

Edition 361 F 04